A Changing Shore

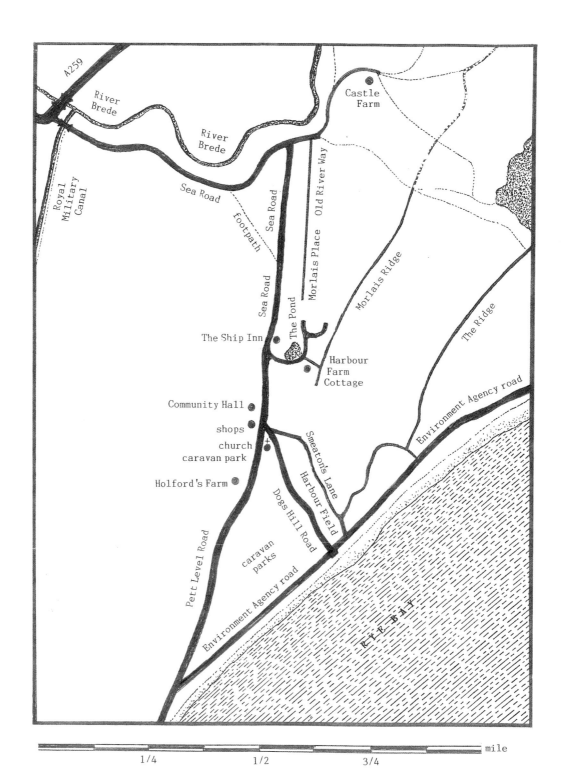

Plan of Winchelsea Beach (drawn by Clive Chizlett)

A Changing Shore

An Illustrated Account of Winchelsea Beach

Michael and Ruth Saville

Edgerton Publishing Services

Pett, East Sussex

First published in Great Britain in 2006 by
Edgerton Publishing Services
Jasmine Cottage, Elm Lane, Pett, Hastings, East Sussex TN35 4JD
Tel. +44 (0) 1424 813003
Email enquiries@eps-edge.demon.co.uk

ISBN-13: 978-0-9548390-2-4
ISBN-10: 0-9548390-2-1

A CIP catalogue record for this book is available from the British Library.

Typeset in Garamond by Edgerton Publishing Services.

Printed and bound in Great Britain by Antony Rowe Ltd, Chippenham, Great Britain

Every effort has been made to trace and acknowledge ownership of copyright of the illustrations used in this book. The pubisher will be pleased to make suitable arrangements to clear permission with any copyright holders whom it has not been possible to contact.

Picture on front cover: John Everett Millais, 'The Blind Girl', by permission of Birmingham Museums and Art Gallery
Picture on back cover: The East Pierhead of 'Smeaton's Harbour' (photo by Pat Littleboy)

Contents

Introduction

This is neither a guide-book nor a history. It is the outcome of a long family association with the area. For Ruth Saville (RES), née Cooke, the association probably dates from the late 1820s when her great-great-grandfather came down to the Pett marshes from Ashburnham; his descendants have lived, worked or farmed in the area since then. Michael Saville's (MVS) grandfather was Congregational Minister in Rye from 1878 to 1905 and his father grew up in Rye and established a connection with the Winchelsea Beach area lasting until 1939. His maternal grandfather built one of the first bungalows at what was then known as Dogs Hill in 1909. The book is also the result of a collection of photos and images acquired over many years. There are some people who know the Beach better than we do, but probably none whose connection with the area goes back so far.

Although this is an account of Winchelsea Beach, we are as much concerned with the general area in which the village has developed as with the village itself. The reader will find that much of the text and many of the images stray outside its boundaries but they relate to features which are so close and so much part of its life, tradition and history that they are inseparable from the village.

Although in terms of space, we wander outside the boundaries of modern Winchelsea Beach, in terms of time we confine ourselves (in the main) to the years before 1945. The reader will find not find much on the changes since the 1939–1945 war.

The images are numbered in square brackets and have captions. Wherever possible the source of the picture is acknowledged; where the source is not acknowledged it is either from our collection or because we have not been able to trace it.

The reader will need to use some imagination to place the past of Winchelsea Beach against the present. The plan of the present village at the front of the book shows its principal features. It is hoped that the reader will be able to put the old pictures into their modern context.

References, sources and suggestions for further reading are in the notes at the end of the book. Information has been derived from many authors, authorities and organisations; the extent of our indebtedness will be apparent from those notes.

We thank in particular:

* East Sussex Record Office, Lewes, and the staff of the search room
* Hastings Reference Library

- Planning Department, Rother District Council
- Winchelsea Museum

On a more personal note we remember with gratitude the information, advice, and support given us in so many ways by: Philip Barling, Ken Hill, Jill and Robin Bevis, Brian Horton, Tim Booth, Sir Geoffroy Millais, Sue Chetwood, Jill and Terry Myers, Malcolm Pratt, Pat Littleboy, Clive Chizlett, Jeannie Norman, Jill Eddison, Frank Palmer, Dr Barry and Jean Floyd, Anne Saville, Peggy Gray, Jenny Stapley, Colin Hamond, Lynne and Hugh Sutton, Norman Hickman and Dr Barry Yates.

Finally, we thank David Penfold (Edgerton Publishing Services) for his willingness to go along with our project and for his leadership in bringing it to a conclusion. His patience and kindness were greatly appreciated.

For mistakes and misjudgements we alone are responsible.

Mike and Ruth Saville
Winchelsea Beach, August 2006

1

Winchelsea and Winchelsea Beach

Millais[1] painted his picture *The Blind Girl* in 1854–1856. Behind her is the Town of Winchelsea framed by a rainbow; she sits beside the Dimsdale (now little more than a dyke), which is discharged into the river Brede near Sea Road, Winchelsea Beach. If some traveller had lost his way and asked the girls where he was, they might have said 'Winchelsea Marsh' or 'by the Dimsdale on Pett Marsh'; they would not have said 'Winchelsea Beach'. There was no such place until the early 1920s. A small area close to the sea known as 'Dogs Hill' or, by the old hands, as 'Thirty-One', developed into the beginnings of the village of Winchelsea Beach. That small area lay at the sea end of what we now know as Dogs Hill Road.

The reader may wonder why 'Thirty-One' and 'Dogs Hill' were early names for this small area beside the sea. 'Thirty-One' because No. 31 Martello Tower was placed there and in due course gave its name to a coastguard station positioned nearby. (The Martello Towers are dealt with in Chapter 4 below.) The explanation for 'Dogs Hill' is less clear. We believe (without any evidence) that it was a name given to a little hillock which may have been the site of the signal mast for the New Harbour of Rye and later for the coastguard station. (We do not know whether the hill was the venue of one dog or many dogs; we have compromised by omitting the apostrophe and calling it 'Dogs Hill'). The toilets at Winchelsea Beach are on the site of the hillock, which was removed in the 1930s.

The Dogs Hill area was a no-man's land, as indeed was Winchelsea Beach in its early days. Until 1934 when Battle Rural District Council was established, it lay partly within the boundaries of Rye RDC and partly within those of Hastings RDC, partly in Pett Parish and partly in Icklesham Parish. It was classified as a settlement rather than a village for local government purposes and as a mission area within the Parish of Pett. It was not until 1966 that the Beach was brought into the Parish of St Thomas the Martyr, Winchelsea. If the family of RES's great-great-grandfather in the 1840s and 1850s sought baptism, marriage or burial, they got out the horse and cart and went to Pett, not Winchelsea.

The adoption of the name 'Winchelsea Beach' was gradual and pragmatic. The name evolved in the 1920s and 1930s when the village or settlement became established. The junction between Rye RDC and Hastings RDC lay near the south-west boundary of the then Harbour Farm. Over half of the plans for dwellings submitted to Rye RDC between 1919 and 1934 identified 'Sea Road, Winchelsea' or 'Harbour Farm, Winchelsea' as the site of the dwelling. But most of the plans submitted to Hastings RDC referred to 'Pett Level, Pett' or 'Dogs Hill, Pett Level, Pett' or variations of these names. It was not until the establishment of Battle RDC in 1934 that the name 'Winchelsea Beach' gradually became official usage.[2]

As the area lay immediately below Winchelsea on its hill, it was natural enough that it should bear its name. Some people in the ancient Town may have felt that the proximity of the Beach to the Town did not justify the conferment of its name on the coastal area. Some might have thought that to use the name 'Winchelsea' implied some form of association, or, even worse, responsibility. There was no formal association until Winchelsea Beach became a ward of Icklesham Parish Council in 1952. Any feeling of responsibility or concern for the welfare of the settlement on the coast was perhaps personal; certainly a few individuals in 1930 were sympathetic when the sea broke through and caused widespread damage. After 1945 much support and leadership came from Winchelsea particularly in the establishment of St Richard's Church.

In Winchelsea all is order and symmetry. The linear village of Winchelsea Beach straggles over more than two miles, unplanned and without any apparent centre. Winchelsea lives on its beauty, its traditions and its distant history. Winchelsea Beach as a village cannot look back much further than the 1920s. Yet both town and village have two things in common. Both owe their existence to the changing shoreline. Both have been influenced, some might say created, by changing fashion or social style.

The original Town of Winchelsea stood on a shingle barrier somewhere in Rye Bay perhaps not far from the present mouth of the Rother. It succumbed to the inroads of the sea in the second half of the 13th century and the new Town of Winchelsea was constructed to replace it. The penetration of the sea produced a sheltered anchorage, The Camber, giving ready access via the tidal channel of the river Brede to the new Town. The success of Winchelsea's harbour was fragile; the flow of the tides, particularly the ebb, was necessary to scour the silt which would otherwise accumulate. There followed a period of growing prosperity but it was short-lived.[3] By the end of the 15th century Winchelsea's fortunes were in terminal decline, caused to a great extent by silting and by the stifling of the entrance into the approaches of the harbour from the accumulation of new shingle barriers. In 1635 a Lieutenant Hammond wrote *Surely this towne was formerly of great note, when (as they say) 50 brave taverne signs shin'd in her, now scarce one signe for a cup of good beere.*[4] In 1699 Celia Fiennes remarked that grass grew where Winchelsea was and that there were very few houses *but the Corporation still continues and the major* [mayor] *and aldermen which 13 makes most of the inhabitants.*[5] Daniel Defoe in 1724 thought it a skeleton of an ancient city and *where nothing of a town but the destruction of it seems to remain'. . .*[6]

The privileges of the Cinque Ports (the Ancient Towns of Rye and Winchelsea had Cinque Ports status) were recompense for their obligation to provide ships for the defence of the realm. It has been said that it was the tragedy of the Cinque Ports that when there was no longer a reason for their existence the barons continued to live on the traditions of their former prestige.[7] Miss Murray reminds us of the *unseemly brawl* between the barons of the Cinque Ports and footmen in Westminster Hall at the coronation of Charles II. Winchelsea's importance until 1832 was only sustained by political influence because of the lingering right to return two Members to Parliament. It was a classic Treasury or 'rotten' borough. Coventry Patmore wrote in 1857 *Winchelsea is a town in a trance, a sunny dream of centuries ago . . .*[8]

Winchelsea Beach and its area had no such traditions or influence. The New Harbour of Rye constructed in the 18th century with its mouth at Dogs Hill attracted the attention of some Winchelsea leaders, who saw the prospect of financial gain and political influence in competition with the Rye establishment. The New Harbour failed, but its physical legacy shaped the development of the village 150 years later.

If Winchelsea lost its influence because of Parliamentary reform, the railway age brought easy access and it became a fashionable place to visit or in which to live. It was much sought after by artists and writers and persons of distinction and means. Down at the Beach, the motor car (as well as the railway), together with social mobility after the 1914–1918 war and the availability of cheap land, all made it attractive to those who sought an independent, informal way of life by the sea. The origins of the new 'settlers' in the Town were different from those at the Beach. This difference has not always contributed to close association between the two. The glamour of Winchelsea has been captured by Millais; its history has been studied and recorded by many and most recently by Malcolm Pratt.[9]

Winchelsea Beach has no chronicler. Many would say that there is little to chronicle. But the Beach and the area in which it is placed have their own story and the purpose of this book is to tell something of it.

2

The Shore Line

The shore between Cliff End and the mouth of the Rother, and the marshes which lie behind it, cannot be separated from the much longer coast line of Walland and Romney marshes to the north-east. Jill Eddison's invaluable book has the title *Romney Marsh: Survival on a Frontier*.[10] That frontier between land and sea has constantly shifted. It remains unstable. At considerable cost man is imposing an artificial stability; time will show whether human resources can, in the long term, maintain that stability or whether there will be further natural shifts in that frontier.

Some 10,000 years ago, as the most recent glaciation of the ice age began to melt and sea levels rose, the area comprising Pett, Walland and Romney marshes would have been a great bay with tides and waves approaching the hills that border them. In the context of our area, the frontier would have been the Pett, Icklesham and Winchelsea hills. The ice age had had the effect of freezing and thawing the chalk cliffs to the west and so releasing flint pebbles, collectively beach or shingle. Some 6,000 years ago, as the sea worked on these shingle accumulations, a great barrier evolved stretching across the bay from the Fairlight cliffs to Hythe.

Tides flowed around the north-east tip of the barrier and so the shelter provided by the barrier left a lagoon. Incoming tides carried sediment. At the full of the tide, when movement was slack, the sediment sank. Over the years, the sediment accumulated, and mud flats emerged; these flats became colonised by salt-marsh plants, which trapped more sediment. Land level rose above the tides. This process, with varying intensity, shaped and produced the marshes including Pett marsh between the coast and the Pett, Icklesham and Winchelsea hills.

The shingle barriers here were formed and sustained by the constant north-easterly drift of shingle, pushed by the waves throwing the beach up and in a north-east direction. Human activity and prosperity behind the shingle barrier depended on the sustenance provided by the constant shingle drift. The story is one of sea and shingle; the ancient Town of Winchelsea and the modern village of Winchelsea Beach, in company with Rye and the whole of Romney Marsh, owe their existence to the formation, and the periodic deformation, of a succession of beach barriers.

The original town of Winchelsea stood on a shingle barrier and the harbour probably lay in an inlet, protected by a shingle spit forming to the seaward of it. The prosperity of that ancient town began in the closing years of the 12th century. It was short-lived. Records show that the 13th century was particularly stormy and these storms occurred notably in 1236, 1250–1252 and 1287–1288. There was increasing concern over the future of the Town, the site of which was progressively eroded from at least 1247 onwards. In 1280 the king's steward was sent to obtain land on the hill of Iham, and in 1283 streets and plots were being laid out for the new town, which is the one we know to-day. By 1290 the shingle barrier had disintegrated and the sea flooded inland creating a large sheltered anchorage to which the new Winchelsea and Rye had ready access.

The prosperity of the new Town of Winchelsea was relatively short; by the mid-14th century there were anxieties over the silting of the harbour and the Town was in decline. By the early 16th century, Rye gained from Winchelsea's loss but only for about half a century. The approaches to Rye began to silt up. New shingle barriers narrowed the entrance to the harbour; sediment carried by the tides dropped and shallows increased. As sediment accumulated, landowners were quick to seize shallow areas, embank them and protect them with sluices. As the process of reclamation (or inning) advanced, so the deposit of sediment increased, thus encouraging further inning. The flow of the tides was diminished and the scouring effect of the ebb tides reduced. Attitudes of the landed interests and maritime interests polarised, the latter blaming the former for the decline of prosperity and the ruination of the harbour. As we will attempt to show in Chapter 3, this conflict of interests in the face of problems over the shoreline had a direct effect on the shape of the village of Winchelsea Beach as we know it.

The air-photo [1] shows beach barrier formation in our area. Although the photo is some 75 years old, Harbour Field **B** and Pett Level Road **A** can be readily identified. The site of the present four caravan parks **C** on the sea side of Pett Level Road is almost empty salt marsh with a dyke running through it.

Two shingle barriers **D** and **F** run north-east. Both have their roots to the west near The (old) Ship Inn **G**. The new barrier **F** is the present shore line. The old barrier **D** lying inland was, in its day, a shore line. Both enclose areas of salt marsh **C** and **E** flowing north-east.

The old barrier **D** developed over more than two centuries reaching the Rother at what is now Rye Harbour before the end of the 18th century. It became known as

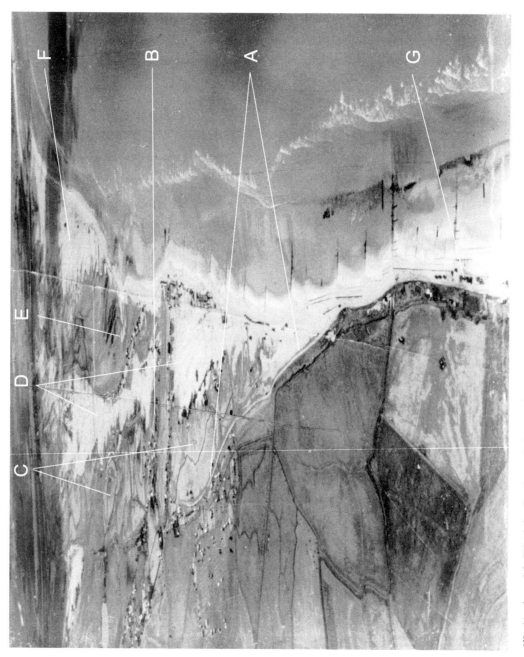

[1] *Air-photo of the Winchelsea Beach area looking north-east taken before 1930. The letters on the image are explained in the text (The photo is probably ex-archives of Kent River Authority)*

Nook Beach. In its shelter silt accumulated and it was colonised by salt-tolerant plants, which in turn speeded up the deposition of silt, thus raising land levels. The earlier salt-marsh **C** at its south-west end carries the caravan parks on the sea side of Pett Level Road; to the north-east it extends as the field in front of Morlais Ridge. The continuity of both the old barrier **D** and the early salt-marsh **C** is interrupted by the channel of Smeaton's Harbour as Harbour Field **B** cuts across them.

Pett Level Road **A** with the bungalows that now line the road, sits on the south-westerly extension of Morlais Ridge. From the sea-wall at the junction of the Environment Agency road with Pett Level Road, the marsh is some feet below the level of the road. Inland from Morlais Ridge and its south-westerly extension, there is no beach or shingle, just the marsh land extending to the Winchelsea and Icklesham cliffs.

Another strip of salt marsh **E** (more recently Harbour Farm and acquired in 2003 by the Environment Agency) extends north-east in front of The Ridge; this strip of salt marsh runs right down to Rye Harbour and the Rother. This has evolved because of the growth of the new shingle barrier **F**, the present shore line. Before it was drained, it was an inlet of the sea known as Greedy Gut, a name later sanitised to The Nook. Both The Nook and its protecting barrier commence at the sea-end of Harbour Field; their origins are explained in the next chapter.

The air-photo [2] on page 9 places the two shingle barriers shown in [1] in a wider context both of space and time. The root or source of the shingle barriers lies beyond Harbour Field **B**. The new barrier **F**, today's shore line, is clear. The old barrier **D** is punctuated by a number of pits filled with water, being the sites of aggregate extraction. At almost the centre point of the image, standing in what seems to be a swirl of shingle, is Camber Castle **H** .

The Castle (also known as Winchelsea Castle), dating from about 1538, stands on a shingle spit. That spit was but a part, or extension, of a complex of shingle deposits to the south-west laid down since perhaps the end of the 13th century. This complex barrier pre-dates Nook Beach **D** by some 400 years.

It is probable that from the south-west end of that complex there ran a sea-wall which protected the Winchelsea and Pett marshes. That man-made wall, which dates back some 700 years, is probably the basis of the present Morlais Ridge. Pett Level Road and the bungalows which border it follow the line of that old wall.[11]

The air-photo [2] shows the change and development of the coast line over 700 years. By 1594 the spit supporting Camber Castle had developed north-eastwards narrowing the entrance into the harbour waters and leaving the Castle behind and of diminishing value. In 1637 the garrison was stood down and in 1643 the roof was removed. The changing coast line had permitted the Castle an effective life of less than 100 years. The north-east end of Nook Beach had been established by the 1770s. At what is now Rye Harbour village, Martello Tower No. 28, built in 1805–1806, stands at the end of Nook Beach. Within 12 years Greedy Gut (or The Nook) with its tidal waters was under pressure caused by the shingle accumulation of the new barrier **F**. Greedy Gut undermined Tower No. 29, 450 yards to the west of No. 28.

With the aid of air-photo [**2**], imagine a triangle with its point at or beyond Harbour Field **B**. One side of the triangle is the shore line to the mouth of the Rother. The other side is an imaginary line through the Camber Castle shingle to the river. The base of the triangle is the line of the river to its mouth. That rough triangle was laid down over some 700 years, the process being particularly rapid since 1700.

The process of barrier formation was followed by deformation with the advance of the sea and the retreat of the coast line. Clear evidence of this change, as the 1800s went by, lies in the loss of the Martello Towers constructed between Dogs Hill and Cliff End. We deal with the Towers in Chapter 4.

The movement of shingle over the centuries from its base at Cliff End and the Fairlight cliffs has meant an erosion of that root or source and the redistribution of the shingle to the north-east. Jill Eddison writes that as late as 1873 the barrier at its root was some 120 metres in width; today it does not exist. In Chapter 8 more will be written on the continuing instability of the shore line resulting in the flooding in the 1920s and 1930s and in the action that had to be taken in the 1930s and the 1950s. The maintenance of that frontier between land and sea remains a continuing concern.

[2] *Air-photo of the coastal area between Winchelsea Beach and the river Rother. The letters on the image are explained in the text* (Ordnance Survey Crown Copyright 1975. All rights reserved 100044881)

3

Smeaton's Harbour

The New Harbour of Rye is commonly, but unfairly, known as 'Smeaton's Harbour'. Work started on the Harbour in 1724; it was abandoned in 1787. The Harbour marked the beginning of the development of our area and shaped the village of Winchelsea Beach as we know it today. John Smeaton was born in 1724 and only became involved in the Harbour in 1762. He was a distinguished civil engineer with a national reputation; he was neither the resident engineer for the Harbour nor its ongoing consultant. His involvement in the affairs of the Harbour was brief.

The conflict between the landed and maritime interests which developed in the 16th century and bedevilled Rye for years to come has already been mentioned. The latter blamed the landowners for reclaiming and inning land, and thus preventing the flow of the ebb tides that would help scour accumulations of sediment deposited by incoming tides. The landed interests resisted these accusations. Winchelsea's decline as a port was rapid. In 1489–1491 Winchelsea's contribution to Customs revenue was about five times that of Rye; in 1513–1514 the shares of the two Towns were about equal; by 1531–1532 Rye's contribution was about 14 times that of Winchelsea; by 1558 Winchelsea had been abandoned as a place of trade. Rye benefited from Winchelsea's loss but that gain was short-lived; export figures for Rye showed a steep decline in the 1580s and 1590s.[12]

In December 1561 the Mayor and Jurats of Rye petitioned for the appointment of a commission. After reciting the importance of Rye as a source of fish and other commodities, its service in time of war and as a harbour of refuge, the Corporation complained that . . . *by the insaciable covetous inning of marsh grounds adioynenge . . . the said haven and harbour of late years are so wonderfully decayed that if speedy remedy be not therefore provided they will be utterly lost* . . .[13] In 1591 an Italian engineer called Genebelli (his name was variously spelt) convinced Rye Corporation that he could make the harbour *more servyceable than yt hath bene at any time these forty years heretofore.*[14] Genebelli produced plans and estimates for the Privy Council. By January 1594 Rye discovered that the plans provided for a harbour entrance near Winchelsea and this was likely to benefit *others of other places.* In February 1594 the Mayor and Jurats recorded that . . . *Jenebill hath most treacherously abused this township* . . . and ordered that *they will no further intermeddle with the said Jenebill nor with any of his devices* . . .[15]

In 1594 Philip Symonson was commissioned to prepare a map of the town and its surroundings to show how the harbour might be improved. A copy of that map is in Rye Town Hall, the original[16] now lodged at the East Sussex Record Office. On that map is an unexplained dotted track suggesting an alternative entrance and approach to the harbour. This track might well indicate Genebelli's proposals which had so angered the Mayor and Jurats of Rye.[17]

In [3] is a highly simplified extract from Symonson's map showing the dotted track for a cut or channel. It follows the river Brede and then the Dimsdale stream to the coast. Allowing for changes in the coast line, but given the positions of Winchelsea, Camber Castle and Rye, the entrance into the proposed cut or channel would be in the modern Winchelsea Beach area.

In the summer of 1698 a survey of Rye (and other ports) was conducted by the Naval Commissioners and Trinity House. They obtained information from the *most*

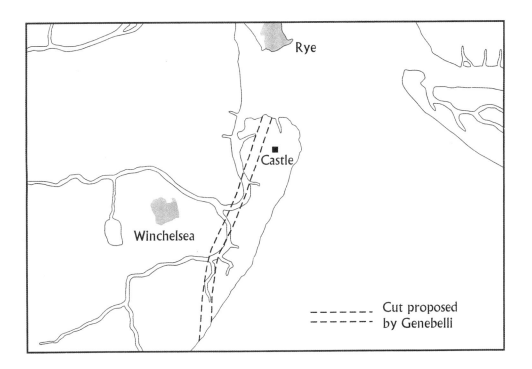

[3] *Part of Symonson's map of 1594 ref. ACC 6394* (Reproduced with the permission of the County Archivist of East Sussex, copyright reserved)

antient and best observing persons dwelling there and then reported *wee look upon this Haven as entirely lost, at least in noe condition to be esteemed for as Services of the Navy as we have observed.*[18] In 1701 a petition was submitted to the House of Commons praying the House to take such course as they saw fit to restore the Harbour of Rye to its *ancient goodness.* The House gave leave for a Bill to be brought in.[19] We have been unable to trace what happened next. It is probable that there was growing pressure from the landed interests for action to be taken as they saw their interests threatened by the old harbour's mouth pressing north-eastwards towards the sea walls of East Guldeford.

In 1720 Rye obtained an Act of Parliament. The Recital to the Act said that Rye had been *a Harbour that did usually receive Men of War and great Numbers of Ships that Rode afloat there at low Water . . . There is no other Harbour from Portsmouth to Dover that can receive Ships of Burthen . . . and whereas the said Harbour formerly so Useful and Commodious . . . has been chiefly destroyed by the inning of the Channel.* The Act provided that *no new Walls, Banks, Dams or Stops* were to be erected. It might be thought that the 1720 Act favoured the maritime interests.

A further Act in 1722 provided that, of a toll (assigned to Dover in 1698) of 3d. a ton of the burthen of ships *for every loading and discharging within the Realme for, from, to or by Dover or coming into the Harbour there*, two-thirds were to go to Rye for the repair and restoration of the Harbour and the remaining third to Dover.

Yet another Act followed in 1723. The Recital included the following: *. . . it is found that the said Harbour may be made more Useful and Commodious by opening a New Cut or Channel from the Winchelsea Channel right out to the Sea.* The Act made it abundantly clear *That the Sea or Tides shall not (upon any pretence whatsoever) be let into the said New intended Cut* until all works for the protection of adjacent land had been perfected and completed. (Winchelsea Water or Channel was the term used for the river Brede.) We have not found any plans or schedules to explain the nature of the works required to make this project effective. It does seem, however, that this western solution to Rye's problems (very much to the benefit of the landed interests, or so they thought) was in line with what Genebelli proposed in 1591.

In August 1724 the Commissioners appointed Captain John Perry (1670–1732) as the engineer for the project. According to the *Dictionary of National Biography* Perry had been a naval officer; in 1701 he was Comptroller of Maritime Works for the Russian Government; in 1711 he planned the canal to join St Petersburg and the Volga; for five years he worked on the embankment at Dagenham. It is not clear whether he was responsible for the adoption or adaption of Genebelli's western solution. The policy, as set out in the 1723 Act, was to make a new cut or channel starting from the river Brede or, as it was called in those days, Winchelsea Waters or Winchelsea Channel.

This starting point was where the Brede turns at right angles from a south-easterly to a north-easterly course. This is shown in the plan at the front of the book. Where Sea Road turns right at the hair-pin bend, a track continues towards Camber Castle. In a matter of yards a glance to the left shows the abrupt change in the course of the river. Although the channel would be cut from this point, it would not be joined with the river; river and channel would be separated and remain so (as it proved) for over 60 years. Until that 'wall' was removed, the channel from the sea was a dead end.

Provision had to be made for the labour force and materials to get from Rye to the starting point of the channel. In January 1725 the Commissioners[20] contracted with John Reynolds of Poplar *for the building a bridge across the Winchelsea and Tillingham channels for the sum of one hundred and fifty pounds*. This would give access to the Castle lands. On 10 June 1725 the Commissioners ordered Perry to employ men *to dig the proposed Canal from the Sea to Winchelsea Channel*. In August the Commissioners ordered provision for *a Commodious Carrying way* from the new bridge across the marshes to the 'wall' separating the channel from the river.

By 1743 (19 years after work started) the two stone piers at the entrance of the harbour had been built, the sluice (commonly known as the Great Sluice) had been constructed, wharfing in the outer channel had been finished and the channel itself partly dug out. The masonry work for the sluice and the two piers was in Portland stone and had been done by the firm of Cass and Jelfe.

The Commissioners, who met infrequently, were not qualified to make informed decisions; the appointment of an engineer for the project on whose judgement and advice they were dependent caused problems: Perry's contract was terminated in 1730; his assistant Edward Rubie took over and it was he who designed the Great Sluice, but he died in 1754. It was not long before the Commissioners were in financial difficulties. The collection of the toll was difficult. Cash flow depended on close liaison and contact with other ports. War or threat of war affected trade and hence the Commissioners' revenue. Money was borrowed from the private pockets of some of the Commissioners. Cass and Jelfe, who were owed money, also lent it. In 1748 the Commisioners were £11,000 in debt; all work was suspended and materials sold.

By 1756 the position had improved but the Commissioners were faced with major decisions. 31 years after the start of work, the sea had not been let into the channel; a wall separated the channel from the Winchelsea Waters (the river Brede); the legal authority for the toll was due to expire in 1765. A number of works were planned, the most important of which was *to remove the Beach and Earth between the Piers to open the Harbour*.

[4] *This 2003 air-photo* [www.channelphotography.net] *shows how the framework of much of the village is the legacy of the New Harbour of Rye*

[5] *An air-view of Harbour Field (the outer channel of the Harbour) taken in about 1990. The remains of the east pier can be seen on the beach with the tide at its foot* (Dr Andrew Woodcock, County Archaeologist)

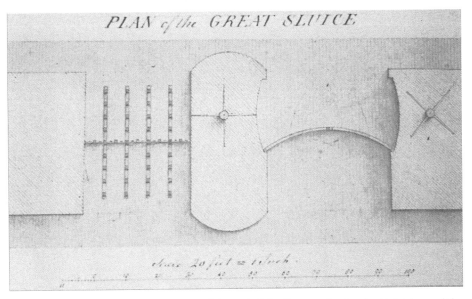

[6] *The design of the Great Sluice as seen and drawn by John Smeaton showing the tidal sluices and the navigation sluice. The site of the Great Sluice is the pond beside Willow Lane near The Ship Inn* (© The Royal Society)

There are a few remains of the New Harbour of Rye to remind us of the works that had been carried out between 1725 and 1756; see [5] to [8]. There are no remains of the wharfage in the outer channel, but the works at the harbour entrance are still to be seen; see [9] to [11]. However, year by year they are being lost.

[7] *The pond off Willow Lane, the site of the Great Sluice, in about 1930. Harbour Farm buildings behind*

[8] *In October 1999 the pond was drained; the remains of the base timbers of the tidal sluice were exposed*

[9] *Remains in 1995 of the east pier built of blocks of Portland stone; many of them have been removed to make a kerb at the junction of the Environment Agency road with Smeaton's Lane. Beyond is the east pier-head. The stones of the west pier were sold after the Harbour was abandoned in 1787*

[10] *The remains of the timber east pier-head in 1987; they are clearly visible at low tide, but each year timbers are washed away*

[11] *The remains of the entrance into the New Harbour between the east and west pier-heads in 1987*

At the end of the 1750s there was renewed activity. Over £2,800 had been collected in the year ending 1 May 1758. Although the Commissioners had decided in July 1759 to open the harbour mouth, a year later (they had not met for 12 months) they had cold feet and recorded their doubts whether they had powers to open it; they decided to apply to Parliament for a Bill to *Impower the Commissioners to let the Sea and Tides into the New Canal so far as it is now Perfected*. Much money was spent in presenting their case to Parliament. They obtained their Act in 1762, but political difficulties were multiplying.[21]

The 1762 Act[22] allowed the Commissioners to *let the Sea and Tides into the new Cut or Channel as far as the said Winchelsea Wall only* – that is up to the wall separating the channel from the river Brede. There was the express proviso that nothing in the Act allowed the Commissioners to let the sea and tides into the Winchelsea Channel or Waters. Thirty-eight years had passed and the question of access to Rye from the new channel remained unresolved. The Commissioners were in a critical position. Revenue from the toll on shipping would cease in May 1765; to let the sea in as far as the dead end of the Winchelsea Wall would present a host of new problems. The Commissioners needed professional advice at the highest level from a nationally known engineer whose recommendations would command widespread confidence. They approached John Smeaton in what seems, from the Minutes, a casual and inconsequential fashion. John Meryon writing in 1845 said that there was no resolution recorded in the harbour books to show for what purpose John Smeaton [12] was called in.[23]

[12] *John Smeaton FRS 1724–1792: bridge builder, designer of the Forth–Clyde Canal, in charge of building Ramsgate Harbour, designer and builder of Eddystone lighthouse*

At a meeting on 11 July 1763 the Commissioners approved two payments to Smeaton: £28 7s. 0d. for surveying the harbour and for travelling expenses, and £31 10s. 0d. for a plan, report and estimates of the costs of works. His Report was dated February 1763. He drew attention to the accumulation of mud and shingle at the harbour mouth and to the pressing need to establish a head of water that could scour the new channel and its entrance. The basic principle of his report was that the waters of the Rother, Tillingham and Brede rivers should discharge through the New Harbour to the sea. The detailed recommendations were for works consequent on adopting that principle. In his view the Rother and Tillingham, united, were sufficient *to maintain a channel from the new canal to the town of Rye, capable of carrying vessels of 300 tons, that the Breade* (sic) *channel is capable of maintaining a channel sufficient for ships of 100 tons . . . and that the three together are capable of preserving an open channel through the present canal and*

19

new harbour, so as to make 14 feet water at neap tides . . . The obvious prerequisites were that the dam or wall separating the channel or cut from the Brede should be removed and that the harbour mouth should be cleared of mud and shingle.

Smeaton's recommendations were included in a Schedule to the 1764 Act.[24] That Act had two other important provisions: the first, that the toll was to continue for 21 years after May 1765; the second, that the Mayor and Jurats of Rye were no longer Commissioners, whose number was now to include Brethren of Trinity House, Directors of the London and Royal Exchange Insurances offices, and owners of land draining into the New Harbour of Rye. John Smeaton was paid *the Sum of ten pounds for his Extraordinary trouble in preparing Several Clauses of the Act lately passed* . . .

We must avoid getting involved in the chaotic years that followed. Nathaniel Pigram, a Jurat and landowner, wrote to Smeaton in despair in December 1764. The latter replied saying that no progress had been made in the works he had recommended; he again emphasised the need to bring in as much backwater from the rivers as possible into the New Harbour. Then he wrote *if the clamours raised by the seamen and by the country . . . are to prevail, I would advise the commissioners at once to give up the undertaking, and spend no more money on it.* It was not until 30 October 1766 that the Commissioners ordered work *to let the Winchelsea Water into the New Harbour.* With the major works at the Rye end taking a long time, and beset by complaints and engineering difficulties, shingle at the harbour entrance accumulated; remedial action by extending the western pier-head appears to have been unsuccessful. John Collard summed up the situation as follows: *…there occurred an almost unbelievable series of delays, caused partly by repairs, modifications and extensions and partly by additional works including sluices, dams and turnwaters all considered necessary to achieve efficient scouring and draining. Orders were succeeded by counter-orders, construction was followed by demolition and dredging by siltation.*[25]

Another 25 years elapsed before the harbour was opened throughout its length up to Scot's Float, below Playden. In June 1787 the Commissioners ordered that no more vessels were to be allowed to enter the old harbour after 14 July. On 24 July Michael Tiltman was appointed as Pilot of the New Harbour and was required to light the lights by night and hoist flags by day; he was also to place buoys and beacons and at *vacant times employ himself in removing the Shingle and obstructions in the Mouth of the Harbour.* His pay was £20 a year.

Immense shingle banks built up at the mouth of the New Harbour. It was apparent to the landowners that their land did not drain well and a body of opinion developed that their lands would be better drained through the old harbour. The town of Rye (for once) found itself in agreement with the landed interests. John Meryon pointed out that the commissioners for the various marsh levels were also harbour commissioners; they petitioned the *harbour commissioners* (i.e. themselves) for that *inasmuch as their levels do not drain out of the new harbour as formerly they did out of the old harbour, they pray them to re-open the old harbour and to abandon the new harbour.* The Harbour Commissioners met on 6 November 1787 and concluded that the complaints were true; they had tried everything (they said) but the New Harbour *is now totally inadequate to the purposes of Navigation and Sewage.* All dams and walls were to be removed. All works on the New Harbour were to be suspended immediately. The decision to abandon the Harbour was confirmed at the next meeting of the Commission on 6 May 1788.[26] On 16 April 1789 the Commissioners received a petition from merchants, tradesmen, owners of vessels and fishermen of Rye thanking the Commissioners for having restored to the petitioners the Ancient Harbour of Rye.

The 1797 Act[27] provided for discontinuing the New Harbour, the repeal of legislation, the discharge of debts and the sale of assets. Section 22 of the Act is of local interest; the east pier was not to be sold but to remain vested in the Commissioners for *the Purpose of protecting and defending the adjoining lands of the said William Lord Bishop of Chichester from the Sea and Tides . . .* That is why the remaining stones of the east pier are still in position.

On 9 August 1800 the Commissioners decided to apply to Sir William Ashburnham for permission to remove the stones of the east pier and in October he was offered £40 for them; the offer was rejected and the stones of the west pier were sold instead. The stones of the Great Sluice, the bridge and other materials were sold to James Jones of Winchelsea for £125. In March 1807 the Commissioners agreed to sell the bed and banks of the new channel in Icklesham Parish to *James Jones of Winchelsea, Shoemaker, for £600 . . .*

Some 63 years had gone by since work had started on the New Harbour; it was fully open for 4 months. John Meryon wrote that the sum of the several times it was open was less than five years; vessels only of the smallest description could go in and out of it; the largest vessel that ever passed through the pier-heads was the *Salisbury* of about 200 tons; she went out of the Harbour but never entered it again.

It is too easy to criticise the concept of the project and the Commissioners. The Commissioners were not really competent to make major decisions; there was no sustained leadership; they do not seem to have been able to retain an engineer of repute; cash flow was uncertain. The minutes of the Meetings show that the Commissioners met infrequently; their procedures were casual and the discharge of business seems to have been inefficient. It is fashionable to accuse the Commissioners of nepotism, greed and downright peculation. It is true that the Mayor and Jurats were Harbour Commissioners until the 1764 Act; it is also true that Rye was in the hands of the Lamb family through most of the 18th century. James Lamb held the office of Mayor 15 times from 1723 to 1756; a member of the Lamb family (excluding those who did not bear the name) was Mayor 38 times from 1723 to 1787. James Lamb's sons were freemen and Jurats. The Lambs and their family and their associates were contractors for the Commission and lent money to it. On 22 November 1758 the Lamb establishment entered a secret agreement for the benefit of its members; contracts for work on the harbour and contracts for the supply of materials were to be apportioned between them. A member of the Lamb family was appointed the collecting agent of the dues on shipping.

Smeaton had to deal with the Harbour as he found it; all the basic works between the Winchelsea Wall and the sea had been completed long before he came to Rye and the sea had recently been let in.

The sketch map [13a] illustrates clearly the formation of the new beach barrier, the process we have explained in Chapter 2. The new barrier enclosed a new channel,

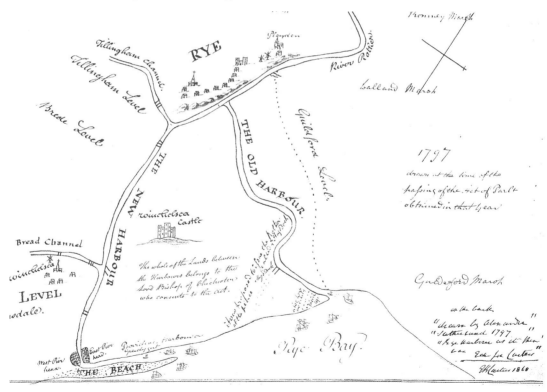

[13a] *A sketch map or plan drawn in 1797 by Alexander Sutherland showing the blocking off of the entrance into the New Harbour by the accumulation of shingle* (Reproduced with the permission of the County Archivist of East Sussex and the Trustees of Rye Castle Museum)

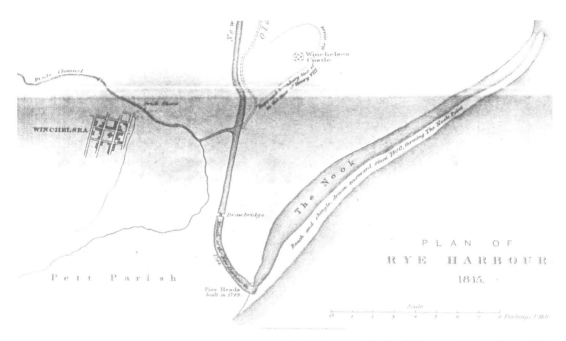

[**13b**] *Part of John Meryon's Plan of Rye Harbour showing the development of the shingle barrier and the enclosure of The Nook in the 48 years since Sutherland's sketch of 1797* (By permission of the Trustees of Rye Castle Museum)

known as Greedy Gut (later the Nook). Although that barrier seems to start from the site of the entrance to the New Harbour, we are not competent to say whether, or in what way, the stone piers caused the formation of the barrier. The barrier moved steadily north-east; Meryon's map [**13b**] shows this growth. Sutherland gave Greedy Gut the alternative name of Providence Harbour. We do not know what use was made of it; its life must have been short in view of the sale of the west pier stones, and the masonry of the Great Sluice, together with other materials of the New Harbour.

To us it seems doubtful whether the New Harbour of Rye would have been successful even if the works recommended by Smeaton had been efficiently and swiftly carried out. The instability of the shingle coastline would sooner or later have defeated the civil engineering resources available at the time.

4

Defences Against the Enemy

Rye Bay, together with the Hythe/Dymchurch Bay, with their flat shores, lying so close to Europe, have always been vulnerable when hostile forces gathered across the Channel and there was threat of invasion. As the shore has changed, so the remains of military defences have been left as visible reminders of dangers past, or have been lost to the sea leaving no trace.

Winchelsea Beach can hardly claim Camber Castle [**14**] as its own. However, the Castle is so near and is so prominent a feature, that the village can regard it as something more than just an ancient neighbour. Between 1512 and 1514 Sir Edward

[**14**] *Camber Castle from the air; the photo was taken in about 1987*

Guldeford built a circular gun-tower at the end of a shingle spit to command the entrance to the Camber, that spread of inland water which led to the harbours of both Rye and Winchelsea. In 1538 a peace treaty was signed between Charles V, the Holy Roman Emperor, and Francis I of France. Catherine of Aragon, whom Henry VIII had divorced in 1533, was Charles V's aunt. Henry VIII and his advisers believed that there was an imminent threat of invasion. Gains in land and wealth as a result of the Reformation gave many a vested interest in protecting the country from Catholic attack. A vast national defence programme[28] (*The Device by the King*) was implemented involving the construction of 10 castles, including Camber, Sandgate, Deal, Walmer and St Mawes. Camber Castle (or Winchelsea Castle as it was usually called) was developed in a complicated and expensive manner from the Guldeford gun-tower.[29] [**15**] shows the Castle standing on a shingle spit.

[**15**] *Ridges in the shingle spit. Each ridge is the result of storm and tide, left behind as the sea receded*

The shingle base is sparsely covered with soil; the land is suitable only for spring grazing. The usefulness of the Castle was short-lived. The sea rapidly receded; new beach barriers emerged. The channel between the widening spit and Rye narrowed. By the end of the 16th century it was militarily out-of-date. With the retreat of the sea, the Castle ceased to stand at the end of a commanding position at the entrance to the Camber, and there was less and less harbour to defend. In 1637 the garrison was stood down and in 1642 the lead was taken from the roof. Insofar as Camber Castle ever served a useful purpose, the span of its activity was less than a 100 years. It was taken into guardianship by English Heritage in 1967, and consolidation work was carried out between 1969 and 1995.

In the 18th century batteries were constructed to protect the New Harbour of Rye. Reid's Battery stood on the knoll overlooking the Brede and commanding the junction of the cut of the New Harbour with the Winchelsea Waters (i.e. the Brede). It can be seen on the north side of the river, a few yards along the track leading from the hairpin bend in Sea Road to the Castle. It is of some interest that the Reid's Battery site identified in the 18th century should also be used in 1940 for a concrete pillbox.

[16] *Reid's Battery used as a site for a concrete pillbox in 1940*

In September 1811 a Captain Gossett, Royal Engineers, wrote to Lieut. Gen. Mann, Colonel Commandant and Inspector General of Fortifications, reminding him that, when the New Harbour of Rye was navigable, *a Battery called Greedy Gut Battery was erected for two Guns with a Store Room, Guard Room, Stable and Magazine for the protection of the entrance to this Harbour.*[30]

If Camber Castle survived, virtually useless, for 100 years, the Martello Towers constructed between 1805 and 1808 were, with hindsight, unnecessary before they were built. When the Peace of Amiens ended in 1803, the French prepared invasion bases and had 90,000 men and 2,000 transports ready from Flushing to Boulogne. The threat appeared so real that the Royal Military Canal from Hythe to Cliff End was constructed between 1804 and 1807, and 74 Martello Towers were built on the south coast from Folkestone to Seaford. They were numbered from east to west; building started in 1805 but the whole set of Towers was not completed until 1808. On 13 August 1805 Napoleon decided to abandon the invasion of England and to march against Austria. By 1 September the invasion camps were empty.

[17] *Site of Greedy Gut Battery on the north-east side of Harbour Field. In 1940, after the fall of France, the bungalow at that time (Windy Ridge) was pulled down and a concrete roofed observation post was built on the site of the Battery*

In September 1823, the Tory radical William Cobbett was on one of his rural rides. He had baited his horse at New Romney and was jogging along when he saw 20 or 30 great round buildings on the beach.[31] He exclaimed i*n a voice that made my horse bound THE MARTELLO TOWERS BY-…! Here has been the squandering! Here has been the pauper making work!*

There were three Towers near Rye; No. 30 (at the junction of the A259 and the Rye Harbour Road) to protect the sluices of the Rother and the Brede; Towers 28 and 29 were built on the shingle ridge at the Rye Harbour end of Nook Beach. No. 29 was demolished in 1822. There were no Towers between Rye Harbour and Dogs Hill; it was recorded that the expanse of *undrained marsh* was *capable of flooding and contained impassable great Morasses* so that Towers were thought to be unnecessary.

The Towers[32] had their origin in the bombardment of a fortification at Mortella Point, Corsica in 1794. The ability of that fortification to withstand bombardment over two days commanded admiration. In October 1804, Brigadier-General W. Twiss, Commanding Engineer of the Southern District, submitted proposals to the Inspector General of Fortifications for a Bomb Proof Tower. On 6 November, William Pitt and

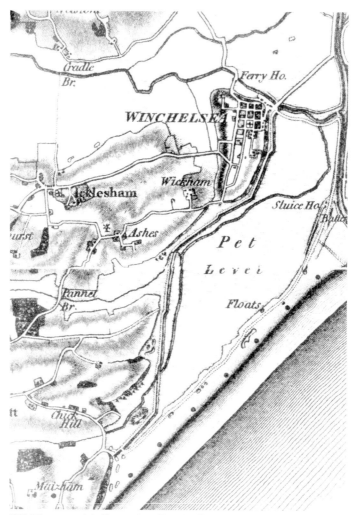

[18] *There were eight Towers from Dogs Hill to Cliff End, numbered 31–38, all shown above along the foreshore. No. 31 is only just visible because of the join of the pages. Greedy Gut Battery is shown* (Extract from The Old Series Ordnance Survey Maps of England and Wales – vol.1 reproduced by kind permission of the publishers, Harry Margary, at www.harrymargary.com)

his elder brother, the Earl of Chatham, Master General of the Ordnance, ordered all possible preparation for the construction of the Towers. By June 1805 it was estimated that the whole system of Towers would be ready by the summer of 1806. Some 500,000 bricks were required for one standard tower; London bricks cost £5 to £6 a thousand. For Towers 31–38 nearly four million bricks would be needed. Bricks were also purchased from Mr. Dalloway's fields at Rye Harbour at £3 a thousand. On

[19] *A pre-1919 photo of the Martello Towers in Pevensey Bay; it shows how Towers 31–38 between Dogs Hill and Cliff End might have looked*

31 May 1806, it was estimated that Towers 31–38 would be ready in six weeks to two months. Greedy Gut battery was withdrawn on completion of the Towers.[33]

In about 18 months, the eight Towers had been built and equipped. To site the Towers, dig the foundations, assemble four million bricks, lay them, mount the guns and set up the magazines, must have been a major operation. We have not found any record of where the labour and skilled bricklayers came from.

After 1815, the Towers were used to house *Invalid Pensioners*, who were paid 1/- a day as Tower Keepers with *no allowance for coals or candles*. They were to keep the Towers aired, and were not permitted to smoke.[34] The future of the Towers was uncertain; by the 1850s there was some anxiety over the encroachments of the sea. They were used to house coastguard officers, although we do not know what financial arrangements were made between the War Office and the Board of Trade. It seems that in December 1843 a conclusion was reached on the future of the Towers.[35] The Master-General of Ordnance minuted *I have always been of the opinion that the conception . . . of a chain of Martello Towers as a General System of Defence against invasion was not a judicious application of the public money . . . which it cost*. William Cobbett would have agreed; his language would have been different.

No trace of these eight Towers remains. Only the name *'thirty-one'* lingered on as a name for a coastguard station, and as an early popular name for the area we now call Winchelsea Beach. The use of Towers 31–38 by coastguards lasted until some time between 1851 and 1861. The Census returns for 1851 gave details of the coastguard families living in the Towers. The returns for 1861 showed that no coastguard family was living in a Tower. They were all in new coastguard cottages.

At the time of the 1861 Census, Towers 32–36 were uninhabited; Nos. 31, 37 and 38 were occupied by members (probably pensioned) of the Coastal Blockade, the predecessor of the Coastguard service. In June 1866 No. 37 was used for a gunpowder experiment. In 1872 Nos. 35 and 38 were blown up by the Royal Engineers.

[20] *Tower No. 31 – date unknown. Originally housed one officer, eight non-commissioned officers and privates. In 1851 it was occupied by George Burtchell, Chief Officer in the Coastguard service, his wife and five children*
(Winchelsea Museum)

[21] *Tower No. 37 being subjected to an experiment with protected gunpowder* (*Illustrated London News* of 30 June 1866; Mary Evans Picture Library)

The following extract from the *Hastings and St. Leonards News* of Friday 26 April 1872 is of interest even though the Towers concerned lay outside the Winchelsea Beach area:

> *. . . a series of the most important experiments ever made on the subject of the storage of gun-cotton have been carried out this week near Pett Level . . . Experiments followed by the hasty demolition of Nos. 35 and 38 Martello Towers. The destruction of both towers was certainly very complete . . . The delightful weather which prevailed induced hundreds of persons to visit the spot from Hastings and St.Leonards, and the surrounding neighbourhood . . . .Those who were present took up a position on an elevated piece of ground about 300–400 yards from the tower and with perfect safety were enabled to obtain both a capital sight of a scene which they could not fail to regard as interesting.*

The only Towers in our area noted in the 1881 Census returns were Nos. 33 and 35. A Royal Navy pensioner aged 72 and his wife were living in No. 33, which was adjacent to The Ship Inn. Despite being blown up in 1872, No. 35 was occupied by an agricultural worker living by himself.

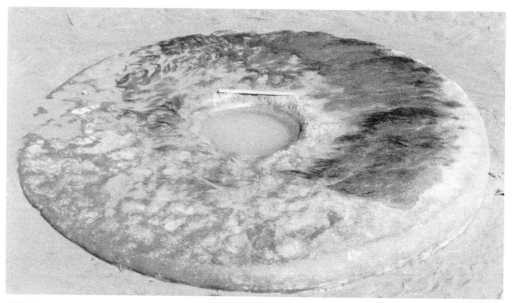

[22] *Possibly part of the gun-mounting from Tower No. 36 in the sand at low tide opposite the eastern end of Pett Ponds*

It seems that after 1861 the Towers were a liability and there was little further use for them, other than for exercises in destruction. The encroaching sea threatened them. The site of Tower 31 was about 120 yards, seawards, from the house *Seaspray*, which stands immediately beside the Environment Agency road at Dogs Hill. We do not remember ever seeing any remains of it.

The years 1914–1918 did not carry threats of invasion. MVS's mother, who spent summer holidays at Dogs Hill, remembered hearing at night the rumble of the artillery barrages on the other side of the Channel and seeing the flashes in the sky – reminders of the horrors experienced by so many such a short distance away. But the years 1939–1945 yielded a different story, although threats of invasion never became substance. The onset of war was common knowledge; the realities of it (at the age we were) had little impact. Dances were held at The Merrivale Hall adjacent to The Ship Inn. Songs like *Roll out the Barrel* . . . and *We'll hang out our washing on the Siegfried Line, have you any dirty washing mother dear* . . . and, more sentimentally, *When the deep purple falls* . . . no doubt disturbed the peace of elderly residents. MVS remembers a minor invasion (from the north, not the south) shortly after war was declared; he and his father were clearing up the school camp (held every year on the land now part of Rye Bay Caravan site) when a small bus stopped over on the Pett Level road; a clergyman got out and said he hoped that Mr.Saville would not mind but could he look after these poor children evacuated from London, just for a night while billets were found for them. MVS remembers that most of them (there were about 10 of them) had never seen the sea before; they certainly had no intention of doing what they were told to do. The day and the night passed without casualties but not without incident.

The air-photo [23] is included as a curiosity. It needs some explanation. In the bottom left-hand corner the river Brede winds it way; from the bottom to the far right of the image, are the straight lines of the Military Canal. The shore is indistinct but the shape of Harbour Field and its curve towards the Great Sluice are clear enough. The junction of Dogs Hill Road and Pett Level Road should be identifiable with the latter following the farming land from left to right.

[23] *A Luftwaffe photo of the Winchelsea Beach area taken at about mid-day on 10 May 1940, the day Germany invaded Belgium and Holland* (Records of The Defence Intelligence Agency, Record Group 373 National Archives and Records Administration, College Park, Maryland, USA)

We make no apology for attempting to place Winchelsea Beach in the national context of the threat of invasion in 1940. We are indebted to Peter Schenk, Richard Overy and Marix Evans on whose books we have drawn in preparing the following paragraphs.[36] There was an overwhelming perception amongst responsible people that the country was under the threat of invasion. The reality of the threat can be questioned now; it could not be questioned then.

On 10 May 1940 Germany invaded Holland and Belgium. Chamberlain resigned and Churchill became Prime Minister. On 14 May the Dutch army surrendered and on 28 May the Belgian army followed suit. Seventeen days after the invasion of Holland and Belgium, the evacuation of the British Expeditionary Force (BEF – and French allies) from Dunkirk was started; it was completed on 3 June. Paris fell to the Germans on 14 June.

Despite the success of the evacuation from Dunkirk (over 338,000 men, of whom 139,000 were French, were brought to England), the BEF had lost virtually all its guns, tanks and other heavy equipment; the RAF had lost 474 aircraft.[37]

Given the situation in mid-summer 1940, invasion of England seemed logical and inevitable. A successful invasion depended on the establishment of air superiority, on the organisation of invading forces and on the logistics of transporting them to, and positioning them at, selected landing areas. The time frame for all this was narrow. It left virtually three months to accomplish this before the autumn gales set in. Within the time frame, options were further restricted by the rhythm of the tides. Rye Bay was to be one of the main landing areas. The Beach with its road leading inland was a focal point.

Schenk maintains that Hitler regarded the invasion (with its code name *Sealion*) as a threat in the face of which Britain would give way. That Hitler proposed to invade England was, in the view of Marix Evans, incontestable; that invasion was just a ruse to procure Britain's acceptance of the situation was unlikely in the extreme. On 19 July Hitler offered peace in a public speech. The offer was brushed aside by Lord Halifax in a radio broadcast.[38]

Marix Evans records that on 16 July Führer Directive No. 16 was signed ordering preparations for the invasion to be commenced. These preparations were to be completed by mid-August. On 31 July the German Navy advised that 15 September was the earliest suitable date for landing, emphasised the dangers of the crossing and recommended delay until 1941. On 13 August General Jodl (Chief of Wehrmacht Operations) gave his assessment. There were two principal conditions; the first that the RAF would have been deprived of any ability to retaliate. The second was that there must be assurance of simultaneous footholds from Folkestone to Brighton with 10 Divisions ashore in four days; unless this could be achieved by the Navy, the landing would be 'an act of desperation'. Jodl seems to have been confident about the first, but less so about the second.

Against this background, we can, with Schenk's help, focus on German plans for attack on our area. Transport Fleet B would be directed between Littlestone and Hythe; Fleet C on Rye Bay; Fleet D into Pevensey Bay and Fleet E between

Rottingdean and Cuckmere. 62 Infantry Regiment would be landed at Camber; 19 Infantry Regiment, a Panzer battalion and a mountain regiment would be deployed on the west side of the Rother to Pett Level, and the mountain regiment would ascend the cliffs at Cliff End and (presumably) Fairlight. Fleet C would comprise 50 transports, 660 barges, 120 tugs and 240 motor boats. There was to be a rapid assault along the ridges of Udimore, Broad Oak and Beckley, towards the hills north-west of Hawkhurst and south of Sissinghurst and Cranbrook. The 1st Mountain Division would land at Cliff End and Hastings, scale the cliffs and push northwards along the hills to a line between Flimwell and Burwash. The Army Corps command post was to be located in the Icklesham area.

If frantic efforts were made by the Germans to assemble this armada in a matter of weeks, so also were the steps taken in our area to meet the invasion threat. We have done no research into the army formations in defence of the Beach area, nor into the measures such as mine fields, tank traps, artillery positions and into plans for the destruction of river crossings.

Concrete pillboxes were erected and many still remain. As examples: there is one adjoining Watch Cottage on Nook Beach [24]; another some 200 yards to the west of Watch Cottage; one on the site of Reid's battery on the north bank of the Brede just opposite the hairpin bend of Sea Road (see [16]); and another close to Windmill Caravan site at the junction of Willow Lane and Morlais Ridge. Bigger block houses

[24] *The remains of a concrete pillbox near the Watch Cottages on Nook Beach. The partial destruction was not the result of enemy action*

[**25**] *One of two more substantial block-houses on the west side of the mouth of the Rother*

were constructed on the west side of the Rother at the harbour entrance [**25**] and another at Jordan's Farm, Icklesham, commanding a field of fire stretching from Winchelsea Beach to Toot Rock at Pett Level. A concrete roofed observation post stands on the site of the 18th century Greedy Gut Battery on the north-east ridge above Smeaton's Lane (see [**17**] above).

Marix Evans shows a defence map of 3 September where German intelligence had marked defence features on the OS map. It shows a continuous line of tank obstacles along the beach between the mouth of the Rother and Cliff End; there are symbols for a minefield and for pillboxes or block-houses.

Although there had been probing attacks by the Luftwaffe since June, Richard Overy sees 18 August as the start of the decisive phase of the air battle; it was then that major attacks began on the RAF airfields. Overy draws attention to the gap between the German commanders' perception of the battle and the reality facing German pilots. Whereas it was the German belief in early September that the RAF had been reduced to a mere 100 serviceable fighters, on 6 September there were 738 operational fighter aircraft. The casualty rate among fighter pilots was causing concern, but even more serious was the serviceability of the airfields from which the fighters had to operate. They were nearing destruction. Marix Evans records that General Sir Alan Brooke (at that time C. in C. Home Forces) wrote in his diary on 7 September *All reports look like invasion getting nearer. Ships collecting, dive bombers being concentrated, parachutists captured . . .*

Overy writes that, by the end of August, German commanders assumed that Fighter Command was a spent force. The main weight of attack was to be switched to

British cities in the hope that the raids would prove unendurable and result in political pressure for the end of hostilities. The redeployment of German bombers from attacks on airfields to urban centres was of critical advantage to the RAF. The battles between 7 and 15 September marked the turn of the tide. The German loss rate of 25% could not be sustained. The failure of the Germans to establish air superiority in the early autumn of 1940, together with the onset of autumn, led to the abandonment of *Sealion*. On 13 September Admiral Raeder reported that the situation in the air battle was not conducive to implementing operation *Sealion* as the risks were too great. On 17 September, Schenk wrote, Hitler decided to delay issuing the order for invasion *until further notice*. On 19 September the order was given to stop the assembly of the invasion fleets. The concept of invasion lived on in a sort of coma.

Down at the Beach, the army removed many of the shacks, old buses, trams and railway carriages; the row of substantial bungalows to the west of Dogs Hill was pulled down because, it is believed, they were in the line of fire of the guns at Icklesham. The Beach had been evacuated towards the end of July.

Marix Evans devotes a third of his book to conjecture. He assumes that *Sealion* went forward and that the landings in four areas between Hythe and Cuckmere Haven (including Landing Zone C Rye Bay) on Saturday 21 September were successful. By nightfall on Saturday, men from Landing Zone C were safely shore and in defendable positions on the hill above Hastings, on the slopes south of the Brede Levels and across the Rother. He has the invasion failing on Sunday 29th mainly because of inability of the Germans to maintain supplies of fuel for their armour.

When one looks at the planned size and nature of the invasion forces as recorded by Schenk, and sets against them the little concrete pillboxes and block-houses that can still be seen, a sigh of relief is permitted that the threat remained only a threat and a short-lived one.

We end this chapter on a personal note. We were married in 1942. To equip our first home we planned an invasion of MVS's father's railway carriage, which stood on what is now Rye Bay Caravan Park. We were taken down from Winchelsea under military escort and collected two old iron bedsteads (small), two mattresses (hard), three chairs, a table and a primus stove. At least it was a start.

5

Some Old Buildings

By 'old' we mean 'not later than 1860'. There were four:
- Harbour Farm (now *Harbour Farm Cottage)*
- Holford's Farm
- The (old) Ship Inn
- Coastguard Cottages

The first three date back to the 18th century; the fourth to the 1850s. The third and fourth no longer exist; they were lost to the sea in the 1930s.

The origins and identity of Harbour Farm (we use this name rather than the current house name) and Holford's Farm are confused and we have been unable to resolve the confusion. Harbour Farm stands a matter of yards from the pond off Willow Lane, which was the site of the Great Sluice (see [**7**] and [**8**] above).

On 17 March 1725 (Old Style) the Rye Harbour Commissioners ordered Captain Perry to build a house for *the Conveniency of himself, assistant and Clerk to lodge in whilst the work is carrying on and that the same be made convenient for such person as shall have hereafter be chosen or employed to take care of the intended Sluices.* It was not to cost more than £120. In 1740 the Commissioners noted that the 1725 house was *much decay'd* and it was ordered that it was to be rebuilt of *Fir timber and Deals and covered or thatched with straw or reed.* It seems unlikely that Harbour Farm is the 1725 house and certainly not the 1740 replacement.

The meetings of the Commissioners from January 1775 were held mainly at the *Sluice House* until the crisis of November 1787. In October 1776 there is an entry in the Commissioners' Minutes that *weather Boarding and repairs of the Sluice House be committed to Mr. Hollingberry and Mr. Holford.* At a meeting at *Sluice House* on 28 February 1782 it was minuted that *Wm. Bragg be paid Five Shillings for the use of his House.* Logic and common sense suggest that *Sluice House* would be adjacent to the Great Sluice. We have seen an old plan[39] of the Harbour going back to the late 1750s which shows a house in the position of Harbour Farm described as *House where a Man lives to take care of the premises.* It is not called *Sluice House.*

[26] *Harbour Farm off Willow Lane built probably on the site of a house for the superintendent or sluice manager of the New Harbour* (Robin Bevis)

Logic and common sense are confounded by entries in two maps. Yeakell and Gardner's map of 1795 and the Old Series Ordnance Survey Map of about 1813 (see [18]). Both show *Sluice House* in approximately the position of Holford's Farm. Barry's *Guide to Hastings* of 1804 says *From Rye return along the wall to the New Harbour, pass the drawbridge and keep straight by Braggs (commonly called the New Harbour House)*.

Our conclusion is that Harbour Farm has been developed from some building used for the management of the Great Sluice, or constructed on the site of that building. But this is speculation.

 With the matter unresolved we turn to what is now called Holford's Farm, a name that was first used in about 1861 and which appeared on the 1873 Ordnance Survey 25 inch map. In the 1841 Census enumeration (often annoyingly misleading) *Braggs Farm* appeared under the heading *Place*. Within a particular 'place' separate houses were scheduled. Braggs Farm, identified as a 'place', had eight houses. There were eight families with a total of 49 people, young and old, living there.

And here we digress into a curious, but personal, byway. Two of the families were Davis and Cooke. Mary Cooke (RES's great-great-grandmother) with six children was shown as a widow, aged 50, and described as a publican. Her husband James had made a will in January 1841 describing himself as an innkeeper.

[27] *Holford's Farm: an illustration by Marian Bradley in A.G. Bradley's 'An Old Gate of England' p.147 published in 1917; the building is described as Old Harbour Inn*

The entries in the Pett parish marriage register show him as a publican or inn-keeper on the marriage of his daughters Mary (1835) and Frances (1839). James Cooke died on 2 June 1841, four days before the Census. His death certificate described him as a publican.

The Ship Inn was not shown in the 1841 Census. The widow Mary Cooke was merely shown as a publican at Braggs Farm. Admiralty Chart No. 7 published in

[28] *Holford's Farm in the 1930s*

August 1809 (Survey by Graeme Spence, 1803) showed what we now know as Holford's Farm as a public house. It seems probable that in 1841 Braggs Farm was a collective noun that included not only the present Holford's Farm, but also The Ship Inn and the cottages associated with No. 33 Martello Tower, which was close to The Ship Inn. As we know that in 1851 Joseph Davis, who had married Matilda Cooke in 1843, was the innkeeper at The Ship, it seems likely that Joseph Davis took over from his mother-in-law when she died in 1848 if he had not already taken over after 1843.

There is no evidence in the 1841 Census that there was an alehouse on Braggs Farm. There was more precision in the 1851 Census returns. The heading *Place* was abandoned, dwellings were given a schedule number, and identification of the building was by name of street, place or road and name or number of the house. Braggs Farm became the name of a house. In 1861 it changed to 'Holford's Farm' But in 1871 and 1881 it changed again to 'Black Cottage'. In 1891 the Census schedule referred to it as 'Pett Level, Harbour Farm'. In 1901 it became 'Black House Farm'. Names changed but the Davis family did not. The heads were Thomas Davis snr and then Thomas junr, followed in due course by his son Jeremiah Davis.

The third old building was The Ship Inn, lost to the sea in 1931. It stood on the beach some 400 yards to the west of Smugglers End. From the sea wall at that point and looking inland, there is a footpath across the marsh leading to Wickham Lane. A little to the east of the footpath there is a dyke running parallel to the footpath. The Inn was exactly opposite that dyke. A terracotta plaque made by the potter, Wally Cole, which was let into the sea-wall marks the spot; it cannot be seen now because of the shingle that has been built up over it.

What later became The Ship Inn was built in about 1742 and was called The White Hart; this name appears on Admiralty Chart No. 7 of 1809. The name of the Inn was changed to The Ship at some stage. That name appears in the Winchelsea records before 1800. It would be reasonable to assume (although there is no direct evidence) that the Inn was established because of the labour force working on the New Harbour and later the Martello Towers. There was probably a constant movement of people going to and from the works along the footpath leading from and to Wickham Lane.

There is evidence that the Bragg family was associated with The Ship Inn. Recognisances of Nathaniel Bragg in 1775–1781 and 1782–1783 at *The Ship and Pier Inn* and of Richard Bragg, victualler, in 1806 *at the sign of the Ship at the New Harbour in Pett,* and of Richard Eldridge (1814) and of Joseph Tree (1820) both of *The Ship Inn Pett* appear in the Winchelsea Records.[40] The Ship Inn and Braggs (Holford's) Farm were all in the Parish of Pett.

[29] *The Ship Inn in about 1905. The lady in the apron is Elizabeth Fanny Cooke (née Hawkins), who married George Frederick Cooke in 1874; they lived in the cottage next to the Inn* (Winchelsea Museum)

The last years of The (old) Ship Inn are dealt with in Chapter 9.

Thomas Davis was innkeeper of The Ship Inn in 1810 and 1814 when his two sons, Thomas James and Spencer Davis, were baptised. At some date between 1826 and 1835 James Cooke became the innkeeper, and in 1841 his widow Mary succeeded him. It was her son-in-law, Joseph Davis, who had married Matilda Cooke, who probably took over in 1848 when Mary died. The association of the Cookes with The Ship Inn did not end there. In 1881 Charles Cooke was the innkeeper.

We have looked at the three buildings that had their origins in the 18th century. There was a fourth and later building that was to have significance for the development of Winchelsea Beach. This was the row of coastguard cottages at Dogs Hill. They were built between 1851 and 1861. We have already shown that in 1851 the coastguards were all in Martello Towers. In 1861 no coastguard was in a Tower; they were nearly all in the new cottages, which were in a row of eight units, each housing a family. There was a total of 15 children living in them. This was Thirty-One Coastguard Station, taking its name from No. 31 Martello Tower, which stood close by. With the loss of the Tower, the station became Dogs Hill Coastguard Station.

The row of coastguard cottages stood almost exactly where the bungalow *Seaspray* now stands at Dogs Hill, immediately adjacent to the Environment Agency road. A similar row was built at Pett Level and is still to be seen, although all of them, except

[**30**] *Coastguard Cottages at Dogs Hill in about 1906*

the one at the north-east end, have had a second storey built on. The row of cottages at Dogs Hill and that at Pett Level ceased to be used by coastguards in about 1901 as new accommodation was built at Toot Rock, Pett Level. There was no longer a coastguard station at Dogs Hill. The Dogs Hill cottages thus became available on the open market. The cottages were badly damaged by the seas in 1930 and 1931. With the construction of the new sea wall in the 1930s they were demolished.

Many years ago we spoke to Mr D. Turner of Winchelsea about these cottages. He told us that after the damage caused by the sea, they were bought by Bob and Sid

[**31**] *A family group on the seaward side of the Coastguard Cottages; date unknown but perhaps about 1910* (Winchelsea Museum)

[**32**] *Coastguard Cottages at Dogs Hill with shrimpers in about 1907*

Cooke (RES's uncles) and he himself had been employed at 1/- an hour to take the slates off the roof. He remembered that the Irish navvies who were working on the sea-wall in the 1930s used to doss down in the cottages and caused fires in them.

The images [**31**] and [**32**] give some indication of how the sea has encroached over the last 90 years or so. No. 31 Martello Tower stood over 100 yards to the seaward of the Cottages.

6

People and Settlement up to 1914

The village of Winchelsea Beach did not exist in the 19th century and the early years of the 20th. So that we may compare like with like, we have had to set boundaries and have taken The (old) Ship Inn and No. 33 Martello Tower as the south-west boundary and the Winchelsea Coastguard Station (the buildings, Watch Cottages, still stand on Nook Beach to the north-east of The Ridge) as the north-east boundary. These boundaries are not entirely arbitrary. The present boundaries of Winchelsea Beach Ward are much the same.

The area was divided between the parishes of Pett and Icklesham; the dividing line was roughly along the south-west limit of Harbour Farm and thence out to the sea. This division is important because the Census enumerations were by parish. To estimate the number of people in our area we need the enumerations of these two adjoining parishes. Each parish had its own enumerator.

The first Census was taken in 1801. However, we have no idea what people were in our area or what they were doing before the 1841 Census. The 1841 Census had many deficiencies; ages seem to have been to the nearest five years; birthplace was not asked for, only whether born in the same county. Identification of the house or dwelling should have appeared in the column headed *Place* but often this was not filled in, or is too vague to be helpful. In an introduction to an index for the 1851 Census, it has been remarked *People still resented the whole idea of a census; it was seen as an unwarranted interference by Government. The more ingenious avoided the whole thing by arranging to travel on that day.*[41]

Works on the New Harbour in the 18th century must, from time to time, have required a large labour force that was temporarily resident. When the Martello Towers were built, less than 20 years after the Harbour had been abandoned, there must have been a short-term influx of skilled and unskilled labour. We have seen no evidence that the area was colonised by the labour force after works had been abandoned or completed.

Despite the limitations of the 1841 Census, we can take the enumerations, compare them with those for 1851 and 1861 and set them against the returns in the 1901

Census (the latest Census from which personal information can be gathered) and so see how, if at all, things changed over those 60 years.

In 1841 in our sector of Pett Parish there were 19 households with 75 people, of whom 28 were children under 15. Of the 19 households, 12 were coastguard families made up of 42 people. Martello Towers 31, 32 and 33 each housed two coastguard families. Three coastguard families were said to be living at Braggs Farm. Apart from the coastguard families, there were three families whose heads were described as *grazier*, Spencer, James and Thomas Davis, all at Braggs Farm. There was one *publican*, Mary Cooke, the widow of James, who had died in June 1841. She was the licensee of The Ship, which was not separately identified. There were eight families associated with Braggs Farm; it is probable that Braggs was a group of buildings in a wide area, owned perhaps by a Bragg; the enumerator did not identify the individual buildings within Braggs Farm.

The 1841 Icklesham enumeration is of little use to us. Only one place is identified and that is Rye Harbour. Three heads of household were described as *agricultural labourers*; in addition there was one *thatcher*. We have assumed that these four agricultural households totalling 13 people may have been living in our sector of Icklesham Parish.

In 1841 the total population in our area as we have defined it, was, at the most, 88; 42 of them were in coastguard households.

Ten years later, in 1851, in our sector of Pett Parish there were 15 households with 78 people, of whom 46 were children. Of the 15 households, 10 were coastguard families made up of 60 people. Nearly all the coastguard families were in Martello Towers or cottages adjacent thereto; there were two coastguard families at Braggs Farm. Apart from the coastguards, there were at Braggs Farm two *graziers*, Thomas and Spencer Davis. There were three households living at what was loosely described as Pett Level including one *agricultural labourer*, James Cooke, who had married Dinah Davis. James and Dinah had four children, including Albert (RES's grandfather) aged six. The Ship Inn was identified; Joseph Davis was the *innkeeper* with his wife Matilda (née Cooke and the sister of James). It is of some interest that three of James' and Dinah's children, aged eight, six and four, were described as scholars. We do not know where they went to school; perhaps they were taught at home.

In 1851, the definition of Icklesham Parish as far as our area is concerned, included, from the Winchelsea boundary, *all the detached houses on the Castle ground, on to Rye Harbour Cottages*. No place is identified other than Rye Harbour, The Ship Pellican and The Ship Inn at Rye Harbour. The households were nearly all coastguard families.

There were just six households whose heads may have been resident and working on the Castle land and/or land that later became part of Harbour Farm. The heads of household were one *bailiff*, three *agricultural labourers* and one *looker* who, with their families, made up 19 people.

In 1851 the total population was, at the most, 97, of whom 60 were in coastguard households.

The 1861 returns were more detailed and consequently are more helpful. Considerable changes had taken place, the greatest change being at Rye Harbour, outside our area. The railway had been extended to the Harbour and the Admiralty Quay constructed in 1853 and opened in 1854. Concrete blocks were being manufactured for Dover Harbour in the late 1850s. There was a small influx of skilled and unskilled labour. In our area of Pett coastguards no longer lived in Martello Towers; they were nearly all housed in a row of eight newly constructed cottages constituting Thirty-One Coastguard Station. In our area of Icklesham, Winchelsea Coastguard Station was established (a little over a quarter of a mile beyond the end of The Ridge). Harbour Farm, Sheep House and Little Sheep House were identified.

In our area of Pett, the 1861 population fell from that of 1851, mainly because of the redistribution of coastguards. There were 14 households with 58 people, of whom 23 were children under 15. Of the 14 households, nine were coastguard families made up of 38 people. At Holford's Farm (renamed from Braggs Farm) there were Thomas Davis, *grazier*, and his family. Joseph Davis (described as *innkeeper grazier*) and Matilda were still at The Ship Inn. At what is described as Pett Level (probably a cottage adjacent to The Ship) were James Cooke (described as *agricultural labourer*), Dinah his wife (née Davis) and five of their children including Albert (RES's grandfather), then aged 15. Towers 32 and 33 were uninhabited; No. 31 housed two households (man and wife, no children) the heads described as *ACB*, presumably ex-members of the Coastal Blockade.

In 1861 in our sector of Icklesham Parish, the enumerator identified Harbour Farm, Sheep House (later probably Castle Farm) and Little Sheep House. In addition, there was the new Winchelsea Coastguard station. Spread over these four locations were 11 households with a total population of 45, of whom 24 were children. Of the 11 households, eight were coastguard families totalling 34 people. At Harbour Farm, there was one *agricultural labourer* and one *looker after sheep* at each of Sheep House and Little Sheep House.

The total 1861 population was at the most 103, of whom 72 were in coastguard households.

To summarise the position in the mid-1800s, in the area which we have defined as lying between The (old) Ship Inn and Winchelsea Coastguard Station, there lived between 88 and 103 people, young and old. Between 50 and 70 per cent were in coastguard households. The figures are approximate because of the difficulties in identifying places and whether or not they fell in our area. On a more personal note, the non-coastguard population was to a large extent made up of the Davis and Cooke families, between whom there had been four marriages in one generation. Both the Davis and Cooke families were incomers to the area, the former coming perhaps from Horsebridge between 1807 and 1810 and the Cookes from Ashburnham via Battle and Brightling in the late 1820s or early 1830s.

It might be expected that the Census enumerations for 1901 would show some significant increase in the population. They don't. The Dogs Hill (or Thirty-One) Coastguard Station had been closed down.

Taking our sector in Pett Parish in 1901, there were only seven households, and no coastguard families. The total population was 25; there were only three children under 15. The only family of substance was that of Jeremiah Davis, grazier (son of Thomas Davis), with his children, mostly grown-up; they were living at Black House Farm (yet another name for Braggs and Holford's Farm). Frederick Oliver was the innkeeper at The Ship. A fisherman and his wife were in a *Hut on Beach near the Ship Inn*; a shepherd and his wife were said to be *near The Ship Pett Level*. George Frederick Cooke, *grazier* (son of James and Dinah), and his family were also said to be living *near the Ship*, probably in one of the adjacent cottages. A ship's carpenter and his widowed mother were said to be *on the beach near the Ship Inn*. In the old Dogs Hill coastguard cottages there was but one man and his wife living on his *own money*. A widow, described as a *laundress*, was also at Black House Farm with her daughter.

In 1901 conditions in our sector of Icklesham Parish seemed a little more lively than in Pett. There were 12 households (including Staffyard House and Catts Land, neither of which have we been able to identify) and a total population of 58. Six of the 12 households, and 22 out of the population of 58, were coastguard families. Of the other heads of households, there were three *shepherds*, one *farm bailiff*, one *agricultural labourer* and one *carter*. The carter was at Harbour Farm and the farm bailiff at Castle Farm.

In 1901 the population in the area as we have defined it was 83, of whom 22 were in coastguard households.

On a personal note, it is of some interest that Winchelsea was attracting members of the Cooke family. There is evidence that James Cooke had become a fly proprietor living in Friar's Road in the late 1870s. In 1891 Alfred, James' and Dinah's eldest son, and his family were living at Cleveland Villa, Friar's Road; he was described as a *farmer*. At some stage he became a *fly proprietor*. Albert Cooke (RES's grandfather) had moved up in the world; in 1871 he had been described as a *looker* at Harbour Farm; 10 years later, his occupation was that of a *shepherd* living at Little Sheep House with his six children including Frank (RES's father) aged three. In 1882 he left the marsh and had set up as a butcher in Castle Street, Winchelsea. The 1901 Census shows that he had moved on; he was described as *farmer* at Place Farm, Icklesham; his son had taken over the butcher's shop.

There is no evidence in the Census returns for 1901 of the presence of incomers in our area nor of any unoccupied properties used as holiday homes. This brings us to a potential change in development on the coast. The Hastings–Ashford railway line had been opened in February 1851, but by 1901 it does not seem to have made any impact on this stretch of the coast. The first evidence of the arrival of incomers to

[33] *There was probably little call for Alfred Cooke (Albert's elder brother) and his fly to venture as far as Dogs Hill* (From a 1911 Directory, Winchelsea Museum)

Dogs Hill or Thirty-One seems to lie in the years shortly before the 1914–1918 war. A new coastguard station had been built in 1901 on Toot Rock, Pett Level. The old cottages of Dogs Hill (or Thirty-One) Coastguard Station became available for rent, as did those of Thirty-Six Station at Pett Level.

Both Rye and Winchelsea had become fashionable towards the end of the 19th century, particularly amongst the artistic and literary communities. John Everett Millais had been active in Winchelsea as early as 1854. Millais had been a co-founder of the Pre-Raphaelite Brotherhood in 1848 with Holman Hunt and Dante Gabriel Rossetti. Malcolm Pratt in his *Winchelsea – A Port of Stranded Pride* has emphasised that Ford Madox Ford (grandson of Ford Madox Brown, the artist who had supported the Pre-Raphaelite Brotherhood) was the author most intimately involved through his acquaintance with authors resident in the area. Joseph Conrad had rented a cottage in Friars Road, Winchelsea. Henry James took the 21-year lease of Lamb House, Rye, in 1897. Ellen Terry purchased Tower Cottage in Winchelsea in 1892. Iain Finlayson wrote that it would be difficult to *find a more comprehensive reason than the railways and the presence of Henry James to account amply for the attraction of Romney Marsh as a suitable literary retreat for his contemporaries and their successors.* Finlayson added that *people were quite likely to get on a train at Charing Cross and arrive* [at Rye] *for lunch, followed by a cheery chatty walk to Winchelsea, and be home in time for dinner.*[42]

The charms of Winchelsea palled for some. Ford Madox Ford tired of the town *to which genteel families come in search of health and quiet which they find in abundance.* His wife (née Martindale) left because Winchelsea *was becoming artificially fashionable.* Henry James was a frequent visitor and noted *ladies in view with sun bonnets and white sunshades.*[43] Albert Cooke as a butcher and Alfred with his fly had come to Winchelsea at the right time. Doubtless, there was a discerning clientèle. Winchelsea Beach had yet to become similarly popular; it would never be similarly fashionable.

Perhaps those who could not afford, or find, a place in Rye or Winchelsea, turned to Dogs Hill, where sites were available close to the sea. Access was not too difficult and Rye and Winchelsea were not too far away. There is some evidence that six building lots became available in about 1908. The Minutes of Hastings Rural District Council record that in March 1906 they rejected an application to build a *galvanised, corrugated iron bungalow on the beach at the point known as Dogs Hill, Winchelsea mid-way between the cottages formerly occupied by the coastguard and the bungalow known as White Cottage.* On 13 March 1908 they approved an application from Mr Henry Blower of Streatham for a bungalow to be *erected on the beach near no. 31 Coastguard Station, Pett Level.*[44]

These bungalows stood on the open shore, unprotected and, with hindsight, vulnerable to the advancing sea.

[**34**] *Henry Blower's (MVS's grandfather) bungalow 'Wrottesley' before the 1914–1918 War*

[**35**] *Clara Butt, the singer, with Henry Blower (whose pupil she had been) in front of 'Wrottesley' in about 1910*

[36] *This photo dates from about 1931 or 1932 and is included here to show the position of the six bungalows developed before 1914 to the west of the coastguard cottages. The first, with chimney pots, was 'The Chalet', and next 'Wrottesley'; the furthest one was 'Foam Edge'. The Ship Inn can just be seen in the distance*

We cannot do our little analysis of the 1911 population in the Winchelsea Beach area because the detailed Census enumerations will not be available until 2011 or 2012. What is clear is that change was on the way. Building and catering for leisure and holidays would be added to traditional agriculture, fishing and coastguard service activities. The 1914–1918 war and its aftermath would make that change dramatic.

7

People and Settlement after the 1914–1918 War

The popular development of Dogs Hill and Winchelsea Beach had its origins in a major change in land ownership. William Lucas-Shadwell of Ringmer married Mary Lucas and took the name of Lucas by royal sign manual in 1811. He died in 1844, having been for a long time a magistrate in Hastings and also Deputy Lieutenant for Sussex. He was the last in the male line of a very old family. He lived in the Old Rectory in Hastings Old Town. In 1803 Shadwell acquired from Edward Collins the manor of Stonelink; the manor of Stonelink was held of the manor of Fairlight.[45] He was succeeded by his nephew William Drew Stent, who took his uncle's name in 1844 having inherited his uncle's estates in Fairlight, Winchelsea and Pett.

William Drew Lucas-Shadwell married Florentia Wynch. He and his wife built Fairlight Hall. He held high office in London temperance societies; branches of the

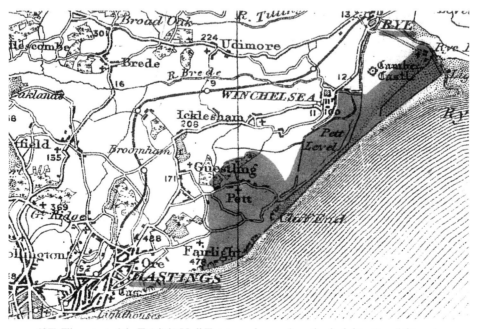

[37] *The extent of the Fairlight Hall Estate can be seen from the shaded portion of this map*

Fairlight Total Temperance Society were gradually formed at various points of his estates. He provided the site for Rye Harbour Church and the Rye Harbour Reading Room was his work. He and Florentia had two daughters and one son. William Lucas-Shadwell died in 1875 in Florence; his widow was to live another 45 years. Young William and his wife became Catholics; they let the Hall in the early years of the 20th century.[46] The grandson of William and Florentia, Noel, died in 1915; perhaps with his death and with no male heir, young William and his wife who, it seems, may not have been greatly interested in the estate, decided to put it on the market. In 1917 land prices were very high, so it was a good time to sell. The whole of our area as we have defined it lay in the Fairlight Hall Estate.

The local press reported that it was the most important sale of agricultural land in East Sussex for many years; the large assembly room was packed.

The Outlying Portions
of the
FAIRLIGHT HALL ESTATE
NEAR HASTINGS, WINCHELSEA AND RYE,
IN THE COUNTY OF SUSSEX,
With a Coast Line of Five Miles.

3,680 ACRES.

In the Parishes of FAIRLIGHT, PETT and ICKLESHAM, including

Mixed, Dairy and Sheep Farms, Fatting Marsh Pastures, Old Sussex Houses and Cottages, with Magnificent Sea Views, Exceptional Sites, Building Land, Woodlands, Ground Rents and Clean Beach Gravel

IN 75 LOTS.

FOR SALE BY AUCTION BY MESSRS.

JOHN D. WOOD & CO.
AT THE CASTLE HOTEL, HASTINGS,
At TWO p.m.,
NOVEMBER 24th, 1917.

Solicitors: Messrs. ELLISON & Co., ⅜, Petty Cury, Cambridge.
Land Agents: Messrs. JAMES WOODHAMS & SON, 27, High Street, Battle.
Auctioneers' Offices: 6, MOUNT STREET, GROSVENOR SQUARE, LONDON, W. I.
'Phone GERRARD 3003

Ward & Foxlow, Harcourt Street, W.

[38] *Sale Notice of Fairlight Hall Estate on 24 November 1917*

As far as Winchelsea Beach was concerned, the two most significant lots were Nos. 59 and 64. Holfords and Harbour Farms were up for sale as one lot with over 570 acres. The two farms included all the land from the Brede to Dogs Hill including Harbour Field and much of the area now taken up by the caravan parks on the sea side of Pett Level Road, all land to the east of Sea Road, extending beyond the lifeboat house and out to the sea. Lot 64 included the sites of the six bungalows built before 1914 and mentioned in the previous chapter, as well as five of the old coastguard cottages referred to as Dogs Hill Cottages.

The sale of Fairlight Hall Estate in 1917 took place when the war had made agriculture prosperous and had led to a surge in land prices. Although the auction was well attended and circumstances were favourable, Holford's Farm (with Harbour Farm) was not sold at the auction; the press reported that the highest bid was £6,650.

Lot 59 (Coloured PINK on Plan No. 2).

A Well-known and Very Profitable Marshland Sheep Farm

known as

Holfords Farm

in the Parishes of PETT and ICKLESHAM, and including

Harbour Farm

the total extent, including beach, being

571a. 2r. 24p.

The House

of brick, weather-boarded and tiled with tiled roof, contains: Three or Four Sitting Rooms, Kitchen, Scullery, Dairy, Cellar, Six Bed Rooms and Five Attics. Coal and Wood Shed, Small Orchard and Garden.

The Farm Buildings

comprise: Two-stall Stable and Trap House for two, Brick and Tiled Cow House for five and Yard. At Harbour Farm are Brick and Tiled Cart Horse Stable for six, Timber and Corrugated Cattle Shed and Lean-to, Brick and Slated Barn with Cart and Implement Shed with Granary over, Yard and Two Calf Pens, Open Shed for four cows and Piggeries.

The house at Harbour Farm contains Two Front Rooms, Kitchen, Pantry and Four Bed Rooms, and there is also a Man's Cottage with Kitchen, Wash-house and Three Bed Rooms, a Brick and Tiled Stable and Timber and Iron Cart Shed.

The Land

includes rich Marsh Pastures capable of carrying and fatting a very large head of sheep. The area of beach is about 185 acres, and a great quantity of the Nook Beach could be removed without incurring any damage. The beach, for which there should shortly be a ready market, is clean and eminently suitable for constructional purposes.

Lot 64 (Coloured BLUE on Plan No. 2).

A Valuable Foreshore Estate

with right of access from the Coast Road over Lot 59, 2 miles from Winchelsea and 3 miles from Rye. The area is

21a. 0r. 3p.

with a frontage to the sea of about 250 yards. There are

Freehold Ground Rents

amounting to

per £15 1s. ann.

secured upon six modern Detached Bungalows on the Beach. Also

Dogs Hill Cottages

(Five) brick-built and slated, and standing on the Beach, now let at Rents totalling £57 per annum, Tenants paying Rates and Taxes, making a total of

per £72 1s. ann.

The remaining Beach is in hand.

This lot offers a favourable opportunity as a financial undertaking in capitalising the Ground Rents and creating additional rents and also advantageously disposing of Dogs Hill Cottages as summer seaside bungalows.

[40] Lot 64 'The Valuable Foreshore Estate'

[39] Lot 59 Holfords Farm (with Harbour Farm)

It was sold six months later by private treaty at a lesser price. We have been privileged to see an Abstract of Title of Mr W.E. Crump. This shows that Lucas-Shadwell sold *all that piece of land situated in the Parishes of Pett and Icklesham containing 571.655 acres . . . and known as Holford's Farm and Harbour Farm.* Although purchase money had been paid, no conveyance had been executed. The purchaser had agreed to sell the land to W. Merricks, who, in his turn, had agreed to sell to Crump. The parties agreed that the property be sold direct to Crump, who thus became the owner of the two farms.

Wartime prosperity of British agriculture was followed by severe depression. Much of the land towards the coast was marginal or sub-marginal agricultural land. Farmers put up their marginal land for sale in the 1920s and 1930s in plots at a price of the order of £25 for each with a 100 ft. frontage. Doubtless, Bill Crump was in the same position as other farmers. We have little doubt that the first conveyance in the documents of title of plots on the two farms would show a conveyance by Crump (or perhaps Merricks) to the first purchaser. Although we have not seen evidence to support us, it is our belief that Crump may have sold much of the outer part of Harbour Farm to Merricks, who was the vendor of at least some of the plots on what is now The Ridge.

The availability of this cheap land coincided, as far as we can judge, with a certain social and personal mobility brought about by the 1914–1918 war. This mobility was stimulated by the spread of car and motor-bike-and-side-car ownership. Mobility and opportunity provided a basis for what has been described as a *plotlands* movement. A growing number of people sought to have their own place in the country. A valuable analysis of the origins and motives of the incomers who staked their claims in the 1920s and 1930s at Winchelsea Beach, as well as Pevensey, Dymchurch and Camber, has been done by Hardy and Ward in their book on *plotlands.*[47] They make the point that the acquisition of small plots *with makeshift retreats* was concentrated in the years from 1890 to 1939 with the emphasis on 1919 to 1939. There was a growing middle class, *a pool of economically disadvantaged people unable to buy a villa or stay in a boarding house,* and it was from this pool that many of the plot owners emerged. *Owning a place of one's own acquired the appeal of a panacea, a way to cure all known afflictions, a promise of freedom, of individuality.* The 1914–1918 war had shaken up society; individuality and independence were more freely expressed.

The sale of Fairlight Hall Estate, and particularly the eventual sale of lot 59, opened the gate for the movement of people into Winchelsea Beach. A glance at the plan at the front of this book shows that the Beach is a linear village. The marginal land sold by farmers fell into three main categories. First, the ridges formed by the excavations for the New Harbour (Sea Road from the hairpin bend, Old River Way,

Morlais Place, Dogs Hill Road and Smeaton's Lane); second, the shingle ridges left by nature and to some extent by man (Morlais Ridge and The Ridge); third, the narrow strip of land separating the river Brede from Sea Road (between the present A259 junction and the hairpin bend). Two other factors that made settlement at Winchelsea Beach possible and easy were the absence of planning controls and the availability of old vehicles (trams, buses and railway carriages) as public transport operators shed the old wooden vehicles and replaced them with steel structures. A wooden railway carriage might be purchased for £10–£15 and be delivered to Winchelsea Beach for a few pounds more and be mounted on a shingle plot, which had cost the owner about £25.

There is, however, a danger in thinking that Winchelsea Beach developed just as a motley collection of shacks and cast-off vehicles. There is another picture that receives too little emphasis.

A theme runs through the years of development of the Beach and this divides the settlers into two categories: those who brought old vehicles or erected shacks and huts and those who built proper, if modest, dwellings. This division was as apparent among the settlers themselves as it was noticeable to outside observers.

Hardy and Ward wrote that these plotland areas were *something of a poor person's paradise with a choice of everything from a cheap ready-made seaside bungalow to a bare strip of shingle on which at weekends you would built your own shelter . . . later business men and professionals were attracted to the informality of it all.* We would only add that retired people and ex-service men were also attracted by the way of life offered by Winchelsea Beach and other similar places.

[41] *Holiday accommodation in the early 1930s, between Holford's Farm and what is now Victoria Way*

Our area was within the purview of two Rural District Councils, Rye and Hastings. The boundary separating them ran close to Old Harbour Farm Lane; land to the seaward and to the west was within Hastings RDC. Rye RDC had oversight inland and to the north-east. Some idea of the scale of interest can be obtained from the applications to the Councils[48] for approval of plans for dwellings; these were not applications for planning approval but rather for approval that the proposed dwellings conformed to certain building standards. We have not found in the Minutes of the RDCs any procedure for the control of setting up old vehicles, or of the erection of shacks of one sort and another on plots of land within their areas. The sites of the proposed dwellings were loosely defined. From 1920 to 1934 Rye RDC dealt with nearly 100 applications; about half of these said that the site of the proposed dwelling was *Winchelsea* or *Sea Road Winchelsea*; six quoted *Harbour Farm Winchelsea*; 27 cited *Winchelsea Beach* and about nine *Dogs Hill* or *Dogs Hill Winchelsea*. When an application was made in February 1932 for approval of the new Ship Inn, the site was said to be *Harbour Farm Winchelsea*. In the same period there were about 60 applications to Hastings RDC for approval of dwellings; most referred to sites as *Pett, Pett Level* or *Dogs Hill* or combinations of the three.

As was only to be expected, these proposals to erect dwellings on empty land met resistance from Winchelsea. In December 1921, Mr George Mellows Freeman, a distinguished KC and member of the Corporation, wrote to Rye RDC *protesting on behalf of several inhabitants of Winchelsea against the proposal to erect bungalows on the road therefrom to the sea*. In February 1922, Mr Freeman and the Commissioners for Brede and Pett Levels warned the Council that the Commissioners *would not permit any water course within the Level to be polluted with sewerage matter*. These representations did not appear to have disturbed the RDC unduly. They replied *that as Winchelsea already discharges into the Brede they fail to see that the few additional houses would make any appreciable difference* . . .

There were early expressions of concern at the appearance of vans and vehicles and other sub-standard accommodation. The Hastings RDC Surveyor as early as August 1919 told the Council that the appearance of a caravan would tend towards *lowering the district*. A year later he suggested by-laws for *temporary buildings, vans and sheds*. The Council decided to take no action. By the early 1930s there were moves in both Councils for Town Planning Schemes. The Winchelsea Beach Property Owners Association pressed Rye in conjunction with Hastings for a Scheme. In 1933 Mr George Graham wrote to Rye RDC to the effect that he was getting up a petition *endorsing the Council's action in their endeavour to suppress the use of trams, caravans etc. as dwelling houses*. We do not know what steps they took.

[42] *'Sunrise' (now called 'Thalassa') built in 1924 by Frank Cooke, RES's father. The photo dates from 1924 or 1925*

The days of the two RDCs were numbered. In 1934 Battle Rural District Council was established and Winchelsea Beach/Dogs Hill was no longer divided between two local authorities.

A picture of Winchelsea Beach in the early 1930s was given by Ethel Macgeorge in her little book *The Story of Two Ancient Towns Winchelsea and Rye*.[49] Her description of

[43] *Photo of the early 1930s. 'Windy Ridge' on the hill; it was the site of Greedy Gut Battery. In 1940 'Windy Ridge' was pulled down and an observation post built on the site, see* [17]; *in the centre Miss Meredith's 'Seagull Café'; extreme right 'Lazyland'; midway between the Café and 'Lazyland', the rear of 'Sunrise'* (Philip Barling)

[**44**] *A photo taken in about 1929 from 'Windy Ridge' on the north-east side of Harbour Field. In the foreground Miss Meredith's 'Seagull Café'; across Harbour Field is the row of eight (former) coastguard cottages; beside them is the little hillock (Dogs Hill?) that may have been the site of the New Harbour and coastguard signal station; the hut on the hillock was used for a little nine-hole golf course; the tea-room and bathing huts are on the sea-shore. Compare this photo with [**45**] taken from the same position*

[**45**] *Photo taken in 1998 from 'Windy Ridge' for comparison with* [**44**]

Winchelsea Beach is cosy and romantic, but also discreetly commercial in her recommendations of shops and of places to stay. We cannot pass up the opportunity to give her picture of time past. The Beach *though as yet only a bungalow town is well provided with stores and tea-rooms . . . on the shore itself is the Beach Hut Tea Room, bright and gay with its jade-green paint and open front, where sweets and cigarettes, cool drinks and fruit are sold, together with many other trifles which holiday-makers and beach-loungers require. A bathing hut and bathing costumes may be hired and – most important of all – the best of tea, coffee, fresh bread and butter and home-made jam is provided, either in the dainty tea room or on trays, which can be carried onto the beach, so that you may eat and drink at your leisure, in the sunshine at the very edge of the waves.*

The developing Winchelsea Beach was not to everyone's taste; some of the properties were, to say the least, in marked contrast with those in Winchelsea and were seen as offensive. Living conditions were, by modern standards, basic. Readers with a concern for public health are likely to be disturbed by conditions at the time. We are looking back over 70 years. There was no electricity (or gas); there was no main water and no sewerage system. Water was collected off the roof and stored in underground tanks or in large c.g.i. (corrugated galvanised iron) tanks; supplies off the roof could be supplemented by deliveries by Walter Alford, Wright and Pankhurst or Anthony Eldridge. In the absence of main water, septic tanks were unusual; lavatories ('toilet' and 'loo' were yet to appear) were earth closets, 'Elsan' or buckets emptied into pits by the tenant or owner, or discreetly removed (by prior arrangement) before dawn. Paraffin lamps and candles did for light. Cooking if not done on a coal or wood stove was done on paraffin stoves ('Primus', 'Aladdin', 'Valor' and 'Beatrice' come to mind). We cannot remember (but then we were too young to worry) that these conditions were cause for complaint or were accompanied by breakdowns in public health.

Public transport to and from the Beach developed in the 1920s. Until 1930 Wright and Pankhurst, who operated from their depot in Tower Street Rye, ran a Saturday-only service to the Beach. In January 1930 Wright and Pankhurst were taken over by East Kent Road Car Co.; they introduced a service (No. 119) to the Beach in November 1930 with a frequency of five each way, six on Saturdays and two on Sundays.[50] The terminus at the Beach for both Wright and Pankhurst and East Kent was at the sea end of Dogs Hill Road. Winchelsea Southern Railway Station had a station-master; luggage could be sent to Winchelsea p.l.a. (paid luggage in advance), where it would be collected by one of two horse-and-cart local carriers from the Beach. Local private enterprise provided other means of transport, at a price; see **[46]**, **[47]** and **[48]**.

Advertising the

LITTLE STATION BUS

at WINCHELSEA Beach

for Station work, Shopping, and other Journeys, at Low Rates.

Sample Prices :

To or from WINCHELSEA Station   ..   **4/-**
To or from RYE Station   ..   **6/-**
To or from HASTINGS Station ..   . **13/6**

The above charges are for four persons, with hand luggage. More than four persons or heavy luggage charged extra. Any journey quoted for.

For parties of four or more it pays to let it bring you from, or take you right back to, your door at home.

Write, Wire, or Call.   J. MONTAGUE,
                                WINCHELSEA.

[46] *The advert for the Little Station Bus* (Wendy Booth)   [47] *The Little Station Bus* (Wendy Booth)

[48] *Capt. Montague's headquarters on Sea Road* (Wendy Booth)

The régime of Battle Rural District Council was in some ways more strict than that of its predecessors. Their Buildings and Planning Committee[51] dealt with about 200 applications or cases between 1934 and 1939, excluding moveable dwellings. The number of building applications declined from the middle of 1936; many of the applications were for conversions or additions or for the construction of garages. The Committee realised in 1934 that they needed a comprehensive review of the whole area of Winchelsea Beach and Pett Level as the new sea-wall, then under construction, had led to increased public confidence. Identification of sites remained unclear; the applicant defined the site and the Committee seemed to have no standard practice. 'Dogs Hill' was seldom used; 'Winchelsea Beach' was almost standard but qualified by the use of 'Pett or 'Icklesham'.

Road or lane names were beginning to appear, but it is not clear whether the names were officially recognised or whether they just reflected local knowledge and custom. Some of these names have disappeared such as 'Willow Avenue', 'Watchbell Road' and 'Watch House Road'. Of considerable interest is the reference to 'Morlais Place' and 'Morlais Ridge'. Jeannie Norman has told us that her father Jim, and grandmother Jeannie, developed property off Sea Road in the 1930s. Jim Taylor, who was a builder, had moved to the south coast from Wales because of the ill-health of his father. It seems likely that Jim Taylor may have bought plots of land at the Beach from W. E. Crump. The Taylor family with their memories of Wales named two areas, Morlais Place and Morlais Ridge, after Morlais Castle (near Merthyr Tydfil). We have found no reference to Morlais in Rye RDC records. J. E. Taylor had been given permission in March 1928 to erect a dwelling at *Sea Beach Winchelsea*, but in July 1934 there were three applications for the development of land *at Morlais Place off Sea Road Winchelsea Beach*. A month later there were applications for the development of four plots in the names of Mrs Jane Taylor and Mr E.J. Taylor, both of Morlais Place. Battle RDC noted that there were already *10 buildings on Morlais Ridge*.

Another site that was identified was *Castle Farm Estate*; this was important in the context of the licensing of moveable dwellings.

[49] *Dogs Hill in the late-1930s. Note the Kiosk with the Walls ice-cream tricycle; Harbour Field is to the right; half way along the road on the right-hand side is St Richard's Church made from converted lock-up garages*
(Norman Card 9 No. 247)

On 11 November 1937, the Committee considered a letter from Captain Montague dealing with what were to be known as moveable dwellings. He noted that the site must be *appropriate*, but that there was no provision to ensure that *we will be protected against the incursion of so much unutterable rubbish similar to some that we have already*. The Committee in its reply said that *no double-decker vehicular structures will be permitted as the same are to be regarded as a serious detriment to the locality*. The following advertisement[52] appeared in the press on 8 May 1937: *Holidays – Winchelsea Beach. Double-deck super Bus to let, excellently converted. Lge. verandah. Ckg. cabin. On private grd. Ample rm. for cars. Near Sea, shops. Accommodation 6–8. Ideal opportunity excel. holiday.*

On 27 January 1938 the Committee dealt with the first applications for the licensing of moveable dwellings. On 16 March 1938 the Committee considered 57 applications, of which 35 emanated from Winchelsea Beach. Between January 1938 and September 1939 there were over 320 applications, of which about 130 came from the Beach. The term 'moveable dwellings' bestowed a certain dignity on structures that otherwise lacked it. Specimens were pantechnicons and buses or trams on chassis. Railway carriages were not really moveable. The Committee resolved in May 1938 that approval only be given to the licensing of existing railway carriages on site *so as to avoid hardship to established owners.*

As 1939 and war approached, Winchelsea Beach was settling down. Many basic services were lacking. To many it had become home; to many others it provided a place for cheap, happy, unsophisticated holidays. St Richard's Church had a good following. Milk, cream, butter and eggs could be bought at Holford's Farm. There were five stores: Suttons, Ship Inn, Pelletts, Uncle's and Gilbert's; orders for groceries could be placed with Barlings in Winchelsea, who delivered the orders in a large basket mounted on a bicycle. The Ship Inn was flourishing and the Merrivale Hall well established. Miss Lilburne's White Lodge Café on Dogs Hill Road and Miss Meredith's Seagull Café, on what is now Smeaton's Lane, prospered. There were many, including Alex Finch, for 43 years Winchelsea's postmaster, who thought that Winchelsea Beach was a shambles. *Tumbledown weekend shacks, converted coaches and self-built bungalows created Arcadia for some, yet threatened to destroy it for others.*[53] There were perhaps few who were mindful of this threat or who were discomfited by it.

8

Defences against the Sea

We must put the clock back. It is not easy to understand how Ethel Macgeorge was able to write so contentedly in 1932 given the troubles and worries that beset Winchelsea Beach in 1930 and 1931. In Chapter 2 we have explained the formation of shingle barriers and the enclosure of lagoons or channels which gradually became salt-marsh. But as the 19th century drew to a close that process was reversed and the barrier itself came under threat. Martello Towers Nos. 31 to 38 had been built on the shingle barrier. By 1861 Towers 32, 34, 35 and 36 were uninhabited. Towers No. 35 and 38 were blown up in 1872; No. 37 had been the subject of gunpowder experiments. The Towers had ceased to serve any useful military purpose. Their future was uncertain or worse. They could be written off. Jill Eddison writes[54] that in 1873 a

[50] *1927 photo showing the exposed shore with only timber and faggot groynes to protect it* (Possibly Pett Level Commissioners' photo in the records of the National Rivers Authority)

[51] *This photo goes back to the 1920s. Note the position of the beach wall in relation to the east pier of the New Harbour, and the huts on the shore yards to the seaward of the pier*

beach 120 yards wide lay between Pett Level and the sea. The sea, she says, *moved the shingle progressively north-eastwards towards the Rother, so that the bank in front of Pett Level became increasingly narrow.*

Before the mid-1930s, there was no sea-wall. The beach shore-line between Cliff End and the mouth of the Rother was of a height and bulk to form a natural, but inadequate, sea defence. As that bank shrank it became increasingly insecure.

The loss of the Towers may perhaps be evidence of the sea's advance. There is more concrete evidence. On 12 October 1923 the Toot Rock Coastguard Station Officer reported[55] that *at 10 a.m. yesterday the sea commenced to break through from abreast the Old Coastguard Station* [Cliff End No. 36 Station] *to about 200 yards west of the Ship Inn and continued to come through until 2 p.m. flooding the whole of the marsh as far as could be seen from the Station.*

On 23 November 1926 H.M. Coastguard at Rye reported[56] to the District Officer at Eastbourne that on 20/21 November *the sea broke through at a point 300 yards east of the old Coastguard Station at Dogs Hill.* The water had reached Rye Harbour; fears were expressed that at the next big tides, the coastguard cottages at the Harbour would probably be flooded.

The situation was reported to Rye RDC, which resolved *to protest against the expense to which the ratepayers had been put by reason of the flooding . . . in consequence of lack of necessary repairs to the sea-wall* [sic] *by the responsible Authority or persons concerned.* Representations

[**52**] *Probably late 1920s showing the break through some 300 yards north-east of Dogs Hill and the flooded Harbour Field* (Press photo)

[**53**] *Probably late 1920s showing the spread of the break through of the sea. The sign advertises building plots for sale*

were made to the Board of Trade, whose Mercantile Marine Department replied in February 1927 that *it had no powers to take any steps in the matter*; they had referred the matter to the Ministry of Agriculture and Fisheries,[57] which had replied that the land in question was *not within the jurisdiction of any drainage Authority and any works necessary must be carried out by the owners of the land concerned.* On 4 December 1929 the *Daily Express* reported that the residents of Winchelsea Beach had sent a petition to J.H.

[54] *The sea breaking through into Harbour Field in 1930; 'Lazyland' on the right and 'Windy Ridge' on the hill behind* (Press photo)

[55] *The flooding of Harbour Field in 1930* (Press photo)

Thomas, Lord Privy Seal, asking him to include the construction of a sea-wall in his programme of unemployment relief.

But it was in 1930 and 1931 that the crisis really developed. On 19 February 1930 the *Daily Sketch* (referring to Winchelsea Beach as *a quaint bungalow summer resort loved by artists and poets*) told its readers that on 16 February a large breach had been opened in the wall of shingle and earth and the sea had rushed in. On 17 March 1930 *The Times* found space to publicise the situation; on the previous day Winchelsea Beach had suffered serious damage through flooding by the sea; local residents had offered to pay an additional 25 per cent of the rateable value of their property towards the cost of defence works.

On 28 March 1930, according to the *Sussex Express*, Mr.Thomas, Lord Privy Seal, had told Sir George Courthope, MP for Rye, that responsibility for the sea-wall rested with Hastings and Rye RDCs. In the meantime, money was being collected by the residents and work on first-aid sea defences was started.

A month later, with the next high tides, a large party of volunteers was mobilised.

On 22 April 1930 the *Herald* reported *men, women and children worked desperately in relays throughout the day, placing shingle against the wooden breast-work.* Another newspaper, not to be outdone, told its readers in *one spot would be a slim pretty girl in a beret and pullover working with a will at a navvy's job shovelling the shingle into a wheelbarrow. When this was full to the brim an elderly woman would seize the handles and hurry along the duckboards to the breach where a small boy in knickerbockers and college cap would shovel the contents out . . .*

The Times of 26 April 1930 carried a report criticising the situation where it was nobody's responsibility to help the beleaguered inhabitants. *Within 100 yards of their improvised defences are workmen busy with pile-driving machinery, but these men are employed by the Pett Level Commissioners whose jurisdiction over the foreshore ceases at this point. The Times* asked why no one was responsible for defending this unstable section of coast; it suggested that the answer was that nobody had lived in this low-lying area until lately. *The bungalows are mostly post-War growths – and that word 'growths' comes inevitably to mind at the sight of some of them. But here they are and the immediate outlook for their occupants is not enviable.*

[56] *Residents and volunteers working at the breach with the usual crop of spectators doing nothing. The north-east end of the coastguard cottages can be seen, also the hillock with the hut on it (Daily Mirror 29 April 1930)*

A report in the *News Chronicle* on 30 April 1930 stated that there had been three attacks by the sea within 18 months and that nothing would be done by any official body to preserve the beach. *The care of the beach falls dually within the administration of the Hastings and Rye Councils. But neither is responsible for the sea.* Something of the attitude of officialdom (and probably of others) can be got from a statement by an official of Rye Rural District Council, who was reported to have said *these people have simply descended on us from time to time, erected hideous edifices on the old shore, settled down, and expected all the amenities of Winchelsea to be brought to their doors. No Council has any concern with the sea, which is obviously outside the jurisdiction of land bodies and the Ministry of Agriculture . . . do not intend to do anything.*

At the annual mayor-making in Winchelsea in April 1930, Robert Nichols, poet and author, who lived in Winchelsea and who may have had a property at the Beach, interrupted proceedings by trying to ask a question about support for the sea defence works. As a result the Corporation on Monday 28 April 1930 received a deputation consisting of Nichols (as Chairman of the local ratepayers association) and R.P. MacDonald, secretary of the Dogs Hill Residents Association.[58] The atmosphere was chilly. Nichols pressed the Corporation *on the grounds of humanity and prudence . . . to pass the work that can be completed in a few months . . .* [and] *to draw up a brief appeal for funds to the public.* Nichols accepted that the Corporation was *practically without funds* and that Winchelsea Beach was outside the legal jurisdiction of the Corporation. (Indeed, as Malcolm Pratt has emphasised to us, the Corporation had no legal jurisdiction over anybody, anything, anywhere except their own property.) *We are not asking you to contribute from such funds as you have but to give your authority for such a fund to be raised.* Nichols seemed to be well aware of prejudice against the Beach because of the standards of some of the developments down there. Some members of the Corporation, he said, were *concerned with some of the erections at Winchelsea Beach*; Nichols hastened to say *we are ourselves exercised in the matter.* He divided the population into three broad groups: retired people from civil life; others who existed on *small pensions through injuries acquired in the service of their country* and a third element composed of *those people who owned cars and came only for the weekend. This incursion is typical of the age in which we live, it would be quite impossible to try and prevent these things because it depends on the forces of nature. These people are of an independent temper.* MacDonald explained that the residents were committed to spend £275, but that it was estimated that £3000 would be required for faggot breast-work; they had expert advice. Mr Swan AMICE of Rye had property at the Beach and was in charge of the advance work.

The Corporation's response on 28 April to the Dogs Hill Residents' Association was publicised widely in the press. The first paragraph summarised the position at the time of the meeting; the second paragraph read: *It has been a matter of common knowledge along this coast for many years past and long before the settlement at Dog's Hill sprang up, that inundations of the sea were threatened, and from time to time have occurred. The Corporation have good reason to believe that the construction of really effective works of protection would cost many hundreds of thousands of pounds, and they are of the opinion that the expenditure of the sum suggested . . . would be quite futile as a permanent protection against inroads by the sea. The Corporation therefore, while deeply sympathising with those residents of Dog's Hill who may have settled there in ignorance of the peril to which they were exposing themselves, regret that they cannot make themselves responsible for an appeal which they feel would be misleading both to those who might respond to it, and to the residents at Dog's Hill.*

Critics of the Corporation's reply were not slow to seize on the words *deeply sympathising* as echoing the words used by the Walrus and the Carpenter in addressing the Oysters. With the clarity of hindsight we believe that the Corporation was right in its decision and in the reasons for it. The reply was patronising and could well have been more supportive if coupled with a promise of best endeavours to influence the decisions of higher authorities. Mr Swan of Rye used his influence with the Ministry of Agriculture and Fisheries to obtain a cheque for £150 from the Treasury in support of the costs of the short-term sea defences.[59]

In August and November 1931 there were further depredations by the sea leading to extensive flooding and the loss of the (old) Ship Inn; something of that story is dealt with later.

The reaction of the authorities came more quickly than one might expect. As a result of agreement between the Ministry of Agriculture and Fisheries and the Kent and East Sussex County Councils a permanent barrier, which would cost nearly £200,000, was to be erected and more than 200 men were to be employed

[57] *The sea breaking through at Dogs Hill in November 1931* (*Daily Mirror* 12 November 1931)

[58] *Flooding in November 1931 in front of Holford's Farm; the whole area now occupied by the caravan parks under water* (Wendy Booth)

continuously.[60] Between 1933 and 1936 a timber and shingle box-wall was built over four miles from the life-boat house to Cliff End with a timber wave screen in front of it to lessen the impact of waves on the beach; in addition, timber groynes were built to halt or reduce the litoral drift.[61]

The dimensions of the wall we give here are our measurements and should be regarded as amateurish and approximate. The wall was 13 feet thick and was framed by 9 × 9 inch posts on 5 foot centres; the walls were 9 × 3 inch planks fixed to the inner and outer posts; the posts were perhaps 20 feet long driven in by pile drivers to two-thirds of their length, leaving a wall about 6 feet high. The walls were braced horizontally and also from the top of the front frame to the bottom of the inner. The wave screen was built parallel to the wall about 48 feet to the seaward; 9 × 9 inch posts were used at 20 inch centres and cross-braced at the top with 9 × 6 inch timber. In 2006 practically all traces of the box-wall have disappeared; the remains of the wave screen are something of a hazard to bathers and wind surfers. It will not be long before all traces of this 1930s sea defence will have disappeared. The wall was breached in two places during the 1939–1945 war to allow the marsh behind to flood as an anti-invasion measure. The box-wall was filled and maintained with supplies of shingle carried on a little railway track running the length of the wall.

[59] *The box-wall under construction at Dogs Hill; the damaged coastguard cottages are just behind; the wave screen in front of the wall has been completed* (From the Fuentes album by permission of the former Rye Local History Group and the Trustees of Rye Castle Museum)

[60] *The box-wall being constructed in front of the bungalows to the west of Dogs Hill about 1935; the first bungalow is 'The Chalet', the second is 'Wrottesley'* (From the Fuentes album by permission of the former Rye Local History Group and the Trustees of Rye Castle Museum)

[**61**] *The box-wall with the rail-track for the transport of shingle to fill and re-charge the wall* (George Roberts)

[**62**] *The new wall under construction to the north-east of Dogs Hill in about 1949* (Probably from the archives of Kent Rivers Authority)

The life of this 1930s sea-defence was short. Between 1947 and 1952 a steel pile, concrete block and asphalt wall [**63**] was built at a cost of £700,000 along 5 km from Pett Level and finishing just east of Dogs Hill.

[**63**] *A completed section of the new wall* (George Roberts)

But still the erosion of the foreshore continued and within a few years the toe of the wall was in danger of being under-mined. A system of shingle feeding was adopted and is normally operated from October to April bringing beach back from the east, so keeping the harbour mouth open, and depositing it at vulnerable positions between the life-boat house and Pett Level. Winchelsea Beach is now dependent, not on the litoral drift bringing apparently endless supplies of new shingle from the west, but on the re-cycling of existing shingle in the bay.

As we write this in the winter of 2005/6, a £15.5 million coast defence project is in progress. New groynes have been constructed at Pett Level and the bays between them recharged with shingle. A secondary defence embankment 3.5 m high has been built from a point about 300 yards north-east of Dogs Hill to Rye Harbour. The planned project also includes new groynes in the Dogs Hill area.

9

The (old) Ship Inn and Its End

We have already said something of the origins of The Ship Inn in Chapter 5. The old inn stood some 400 yards west of the junction of the Environment Agency road with Pett Level Road.

[64] *The Ship Inn in the late 1920s. The two boats on the shore give some indication of the distance between the inn and the high tide marks. Beyond the inn is the cottage which may have been built in association with Martello Tower No. 33* (Wendy Booth)

Thomas Davis, who was at Braggs Farm in 1841, had been the publican of The Ship in the period 1810–1814. It was between his children and those of James Cooke that there were four marriages in one generation. The association of the two familes with The Ship is remarkable. James Cooke, who had come down from Ashburnham, probably in the late 1820s, was the innkeeper in the years running up to 1841. His widow, Mary, probably succeeded him when he died in early June 1841. Mary Cooke died in 1848. At the time of the 1851 Census Joseph Davis and his wife Matilda (née Cooke and the daughter of James) were at The Ship. Perhaps Joseph had taken over

[**65**] *The Ship Inn in the 1920s with the 'road' to Pett Level* (Goulden, Bexhill)

from his mother-in-law. The Census returns for 1861 and 1871 show Joseph and Matilda still running The Ship. In 1881 Charles Cooke (a nephew of Matilda Davis and grandson of James) was the innkeeper.

At the risk of digression, it is of some interest to say something of Charles's wife, Eliza. She was a Wicks; her father was a coastguard who probably served in Ireland. The family does not appear in the 1841 Census. In 1851 they were in No. 33 Martello Tower with five children aged from 11 to two. There was another coastguard family in the Tower with four children. Elizabeth Wicks is shown as aged nine and as having been born in Waterford. Her younger brother and sister are both shown as having been born in Pett; they were almost certainly born in the Tower. The site of the Tower was immediately adjoining The Ship, but the Tower itself was probably some 100 yards seaward of the inn. Charles and Eliza were married on 13 October 1873 at Pett. Their son, Reg Cooke (1890–1965), farmer and naturalist, in his reminiscences published in the *Hastings and St. Leonards Observer* on 28 June 1969 remembered that his father had kept The Ship for several years up to 1887. The full text of these fascinating reminiscences is reproduced in John Taylor's book on the village of Pett.[62] *It was,* Reg Cooke wrote, *a rather remarkable place. Almost everyone met in there, and there were some characters – artists, sculptors, authors and others, some of whom became famous … My mother has told me that when father and she kept The Ship, their patrons were mainly Coastguards, and the officers had to have a separate room. They were not allowed to drink with the men. Whisky was 4d. a quarter – about two doubles.*

George Hickman was landlord from 1925 to January 1937. We are indebted to the Hickman family for much information on the Inn. (Norman Hickman is George's grandson.) In 1929 Whitbread bought out Mackeson, Frederick Leney & Sons. The Hickmans used to provide meals for visitors; amongst those who signed the visitors' book were Henry Savage the author, Gracie Fields, James Robertson Justice and Geoffrey de Havilland. Stories about The Ship abound and have entered local folk-lore. We exercise restraint and only retail the one about de Haviland. On one occcasion he phoned 'Lady Hicky', as he called Mrs Hickman, from Croydon and ordered a savoury omelette in half an hour's time. He arrived punctually, by air, and landed on the sand; he had his meal, flew off and came down in the evening in his Ferrari (or was it a Bugatti?). The atmosphere was distinctly bohemian. Another informant told us of chorus girls doing work-outs on the sand. A measure of privacy was assured in that the Inn was way off the policeman's beat and (to some extent) away from the public gaze.

[66] *The Ship Inn in the 1920s facing the sea. Already faggot groynes have been placed to protect the building from the waves* (Goulden, Bexhill)

[67] *George Hickman, landlord of The Ship Inn 1925–1937. The photo was taken before 1931* (Norman Hickman)

[68] *Mrs. Hickman, before 1931* (Norman Hickman)

[69] *A print by, it is believed, D. Laing inspired by the 1931 gales and the loss of The Ship*

The life and the traditions of The (old) Ship Inn came to an end as 1931 drew to a close. The stormy weather that had beset Winchelsea Beach in 1930 came again in August and November 1931. The interest and imagination of the press which had been captured in 1930 were further stimulated; Winchelsea Beach and The Ship Inn received national publicity.[63]

On 18 August 1931, a newspaper (not identified) reported that *the 450-year old Ship Inn was being pounded by the waves, the foundations have been undermined and the famous landmark is expected to slide into the sea.* The *News Chronicle* told its readers that the doors and windows of the inn were being barricaded, *but it was not expected there would be such a night of terror as was experienced last night.* The *News Chronicle* added that *despite the general lightheartedness it is apparent that sooner or later Winchelsea Beach will disappear.* The Herald, on the same date, reported that the *two thousand* [sic] people who live in the *bungalow town on Winchelsea Beach are wondering whether they will have any homes when another night comes.* The *Herald* found that *the 400-year-old smugglers' inn – the Ship – has 12ft. of water in its cellars.* The *Daily Mirror* said that *residents of the Ship Hotel Winchelsea Sussex and bungalow residents are in terror because of the high seas . . . Yesterday afternoon waves 50 feet in height were breaking near the hotel.*

[70] *After the November 1931 gale* (Norman Hickman)

[**71**] *But the postman calls* (Norman Hickman)

The extent of the damage to The Ship in the August gale is not known; it is unlikely that the Hickmans were deterred from opening for business. The night is remembered by MVS, who was in a tent at a school camp on land now used by Rye Bay Caravan Park. Everyone had to get out of the tents and spend the night in a lean-to adjoining the railway carriage used as headquarters for the camp. It was all a bit of

[**72**] *A terracotta plaque made by Wally Cole and let into the sea-wall in about 1953. It can no longer be seen as the shingle has been built up to the top of the wall*

[73] *The (new) Ship Inn with the Merrivale Hall behind and reflected in the pool, the remains of the Great Sluice. Date of photo unknown – perhaps late 1940s* (Photocrom Co. Ltd 75401)

a lark. But for residents and the Hickmans the November gale was much worse. The *Daily Herald* in its issue of 11 November 1931 told its readers that at 11 p.m. the previous night the sea wall protecting houses at Winchelsea Beach was burst by the force of terrific seas . . . *mountainous seas broke on the Ship Inn . . . shattering the wooden balcony . . . after the peak of the midnight tide the Ship Inn was a distressing sight . . . the ground floor cellar was wrecked and dozens of barrels of beer were swept away.*

It was thought that it was not worthwhile re-building The Ship. On 1 February 1932 Rye RDC approved building plans for an Inn *at Harbour Farm Winchelsea* submitted by T. Leney and Son. The licence was transferred to the new premises (confirmation by phone) and The (new) Ship Inn opened for business on the same evening.

There are no remains of The (old) Ship Inn to remind us of a building that stood for about 200 years and which played such an important part in the history of our area other than the plaque shown in [72].

The old inn was pulled down and the timbers used to build the Ship Inn Stores adjacent to the inn. At the back of The (new) Ship Inn the Merrivale Hall was built, a well-remembered venue for dances in the late 1930s.

10

The Lifeboat Disaster of 1928

No account of Winchelsea Beach can ignore this local disaster. Outside the boundaries of the village, and about half way between Dogs Hill and the mouth of the Rother, stands the old lifeboat house, a reminder to residents and visitors of the tragic loss experienced by the neighbouring village of Rye Harbour in November 1928. On 15 November the *Mary Stanford*, the Rye Harbour lifeboat, capsized and her crew of 17 were drowned.

The story of what happened on that November day has been well told by Geoff Hutchinson[64] and Richard Tollett.[65] In addition, there is much official information in issues of *The Lifeboat,* the journal of the National Lifeboat Institution. We are indebted to these sources.

[74] *The old lifeboat house from which the Mary Stanford was launched on 15 November 1928 and to which she did not return* (F.B. Laitwood)

The *Mary Stanford* was a pulling-and-sailing, non-self-righting, lifeboat of the 'Liverpool' type built in 1916. She was 38 feet long and weighed over 4½ tons. The oars were 15 feet long. The first boat of this name was given to the Rye lifeboat station, which from 1881 operated from Camber Sands. The Rye station was closed and the duties taken over by the Rye Harbour station in 1910. The second *Mary Stanford* came on station in 1916.

The *Mary Stanford* had a crew of 17, the coxswain and 16. The lifeboat house was 1½ miles from the village of Rye Harbour. The reader may ask why the lifeboat was housed at this remote spot and not at the village. The reason was that because of the tides the launching of the lifeboat into the river could not be relied on. At low tide there would be insufficient depth of water. Adverse winds and an incoming tide could make it almost impossible to get a pulling–sailing lifeboat down the river and out to sea. On the other hand, launching the lifeboat on a low-lying shore presented real difficulties; there was no high sloping slipway down which the boat could run straight into the sea. The lifeboat had to be manhandled over greasy skids to get her down the beach and across the sand. The lower the tide, the more difficult would be the launching process. It is estimated that up to 60 people would assist in the launching.

The reader may also be aghast that the *Mary Stanford* was a non-self-righting boat. *The Lifeboat* carried an article on this issue.[66] A non-self-righting boat was as equally likely to capsize as a self-righter. The power to self-right was obtained by two chambers or end-boxes and by a heavy keel weighing from one-third to one-fifth of the boat's total weight. The end-boxes made the self-righter less easy to handle in heavy weather. The heavy keel would make launching on our flat tidal shore much more difficult.

The crew was experienced. After the disaster, the Wreck Commissioner's Court was asked how many times the *Mary Stanford* had been put to use and had she proved a good sea boat in rough weather. The Court said that she had been launched on practice 47 times and 15 times on active service. She had proved to be a good sea boat upon all occasions, several of the services under conditions similar to those prevailing at the time of the disaster. At no time had the crew expressed dis-satisfaction with the boat.[67]

The reader must consider the disaster against the background set out above. At 4.50 a.m. on 15 November 1928 Rye Harbour Coastguard Station received a message from North Foreland Radio Station:

Steamer Alice of Riga leaking – danger – drifting SW to W 8 miles from Dungeness 0430 [i.e. 4.30 a.m.]

She had been in collision with a German vessel SS *Smyrna,* had lost her rudder and had a hole torn in her side. *Smyrna* was unable to rescue the crew of the *Alice* in the dark and with the high sea running. The maroon was sounded at Rye Harbour just after 5 a.m. The crew and the launchers had to get from the village to the lifeboat house, a distance of 1½ miles, in the gale and driving rain.

The had to be lugged across the beach and over the sand using greased skids. She was launched, at the third attempt,[68] at about 6.45 a.m. at approximately low water.

[75] *The memorial in Rye Harbour churchyard*

The wind was SSW Force 8–10 (39–63 mph), a full gale, with a *very high rough broken sea*. The crew would be already soaked in the struggles to launch and then to get into the boat. In the event the crew of the *Alice* was saved by the *Smyrna* as it was getting light and the services of the *Mary Stanford* were not needed. This message reached North Foreland Radio Station and Ramsgate Coastguard Station at 6.12 a.m. The Rye Harbour Coastguard Station received this message at 6.50 a.m., 38 minutes later and it was immediately transmitted to the lifeboat house.[69] The recall signal was not seen by the crew because of the appalling weather conditions at the time. The *Mary Stanford* was seen by SS *Halton* at 9.30 a.m. about 3 miles WSW of Dungeness. She made for the Harbour but capsized at about 10.30 a.m. when she was about 1½ miles SSE from the Rye Coastguard look-out hut. There were no survivors.

Richard Tollett writes that the main topic of conversation was what was the lifeboat doing in the position where it capsized. The popular view, he says, was that they were looking for two members of the crew who had been washed overboard. It might be expected that the lifeboat would seek shelter in the lee of Dungeness or go in to Folkestone until the weather quietened. But all is conjecture. The crew had been at sea for over three hours and were probably nearly exhausted, the tide was approaching the full and to seek the shelter and calm of the Harbour itself seemed to be the correct decision; to approach the lifeboat house, on a lee shore, in a full gale, may well have seemed beyond their strength and capacity. As for the capsize, we might wonder whether the *Mary Stanford* had shipped much water and was unstable; the gale and the sea would have been on her port quarter and she may have been caught in a gust and an exceptionally large wave and broached to.

The 17 men who lost their lives were Herbert Head, the Coxswain, and his two sons James and John; Joseph Stonham, the second Coxswain; Henry Cutting and his two brothers Robert and Albert; three Pope brothers; two Clark brothers; Morriss and Arthur Downey, cousins; Herbert Smith, Walter Igglesden and Charles Southerden; 15 of them were buried in Rye Harbour Churchyard on 20 November. The body of Henry Cutting was not found until three months later; that of John Head (aged 17) was never recovered.

A report in *The Times* of 21 November said: *Rye Harbour seems remote from the homely old town on a hill two miles away, and the hamlet, thinly spread where the marshes meet the lonely shore, was a desolate place in the storm swept days of sorrow last week.*

The lifeboat house, never again used for that purpose, stands as a bleak and lonely memorial to lives lost so that others might live, but on what proved to be a needless mission.

11

St Richard's Church

In view of the way in which Winchelsea Beach developed, it is not surprising that there was no church until the mid-1930s. An account of its beginnings is in the Notes of the Rector of Pett dated July 1935, three copies of which were found (together with other documents) in a drawer in the Vestry in November 2000. The author of these Notes was the Revd H.E. Moxon, Rector of Pett. They had been unearthed in 1967 by the then Rector, the Revd E.A. Parkins, after enquiry by Mrs Craddock of Winchelsea Beach. We were privileged to be able to read these old records and to summarise their contents before the Rector of Winchelsea deposited them at the East Sussex Record Office in Lewes.[70]

We have already emphasised that Winchelsea Beach was divided between the Parishes of Pett and Icklesham for civil purposes. The ecclesiastical division since 1903 was between Pett and Rye Harbour. Roughly, the area to the seaward and west of the SW boundary of Harbour Farm was within the purview of Pett. As we have shown, the burials, baptisms and marriages of the Cooke and Davis families in the 19th century were performed at Pett. Early in 1935 Pett Parish had acquired a disused Admiralty building at Pett Level and converted it into the Church of St Nicholas. The interest in, and response to, that initiative prompted a similar experiment at Winchelsea Beach. The Rector pointed out that there were two problems: to find a place of worship and to find a priest who would help and act as Moxon's representative on the spot. The opportunity arose to buy lock-up garages beside the recreation ground (Harbour Field) from Mr Walter Merricks for £175. It is believed that the garages were originally a barn on a Merricks' farm; it was brought down to the Beach by him for conversion into lock-up garages as a business venture.

At the time of writing his Notes, the Rector recorded that £120 towards the purchase price had been collected, which included £50 from the Sussex Church Builders Fund. The balance had been collected by Miss E.P. Holmes, to whom Moxon recorded his gratitude for her *energetic and enthusiastic support*. Moxon recorded that the Vicar of Rye Harbour had given his consent to the endeavours to minister to

[76] *The former lock-up garages on Dogs Hill Road converted into the Church of St Richard in 1935*
(Press photo)

his parishioners at the Beach. After the war relationships with the Parish of Rye Harbour became a major issue which had to be referred to the Bishop of Chichester. Battle RDC agreed to the use of the old garages as a temporary church. W.P. Cole with staff and students of Hastings School of Art carried out the scheme of decorations; needlework was done by Mrs Burke of Winchelsea and her helpers and also by the Church Needlework Party of St Leonard's. A bell was provided and hung *in memory of a sister*; the concrete altar was made by Mr Gould of Messrs Simpson of Rye Harbour. The Rector's note ended *above all we are indebted to Mr. and Mrs. Gayford, who in addition to the caretaking, have done far more for the church than it is possible to acknowledge.* The Register of Church Services started on Sunday 15 September 1935. On Saturday 4 July 1936 the Register recorded the dedication of the *Chapel of St. Richard and its ornaments* and the entry was signed by the Bishop of Lewes.

Although the Register records the first service in September 1935, it seems that there were services in July and August. There are references to a Mr Dachtler, assistant curate of St Thomas, Upper Clapton, giving up two weeks of his holiday to make a start. On 28 July the Revd W. Berner of South Tottenham, who had had Australian experience, was to come for several weeks and would be staying at *Miss Meredith's Seagull Café.*

[77] *The dedication of the Chapel of St Richard by the Bishop of Lewes 4 July 1936. A press report referred to the Church converted from six lock-up garages, with an altar of concrete, whitewashed wooden walls and candle lighting* (From St Richard's records)

The site of the old Church is still visible half way along Dogs Hill Road on the edge of Harbour Field. With the outbreak of war, the last service was held on 14 July 1940. A note in the Register read:

School children were evacuated from Winchelsea Beach on Sunday July 21st. No services were held on that day. Evacuation of civilians was completed on Wednesday July 24th.

The Church was damaged by enemy action. A pamphlet written in 1955 by Mr Chaning-Pearce, of Winchelsea, then Chairman of the Church Committee, recorded that war damage had been repaired, the Church blessed and re-opened and that services had been resumed in 1949 and were taken by the Rector of Pett (Revd R.C. Wood) until he retired in 1953. The living fell vacant and services ceased. The new Register commenced with a re-dedication service on 10 July 1955 and services were resumed under a 'Lady Missioner' as 'Missioner-in-Charge'; the lady was Miss C.M. Biddle, who lived at *Harbour Bank* at the junction of Smeaton's Lane and Dogs Hill Road. Many services in the winter seem to have been taken by her and held at her home because of dampness in the Church. Chaning-Pearce's pamphlet said that the area was designated a 'mission area'; average attendance at Sunday services was 55, but 130 at the peak of the summer.

[78] *The interior of the old St Richard's Church* (From St Richard's records)

It seems that Melville Chaning-Pearce (with Miss Biddle) was responsible for the launching of an appeal. He recorded that in October 1955 the site for the new church had been purchased for £275. Between 1955 and 1961 planning for the new church gathered momentum. The foundation stone was laid by Miss Biddle on 29 September 1961. The architect was Duncan Wylson of Rye and of the firm, Wylson and Cox. The builders were Padden and Durrant. There were difficulties over the project as enthusiasm was not always tempered by the discipline of available finance. On 1 November 1962 the new Church was dedicated by the Archdeacon of Hastings; 268 people attended.

The *Sussex Express and County Herald* of 30 August 1963 carried a report on the Church. It seated 70; the tower roof was anglo-saxon in form known as Rhenish Helm spire; the pulpit carving came from a Coptic Church in Ethiopia. There had been a grand holiday fête on 21 August as part of an effort to raise £1800 to pay off the building debt of the new church. The altar was the original concrete one made for the old church. The kneelers were made by friends of St Richard's and the two large kneelers near the altar by Winchelsea Beach WI. (We have been told that the two-manual organ came from Rochester Cathedral.) This report continued that the church had no priest but that *since July 1, the Rev. Father John Legg, fresh from ministering the diocese of North West Australia had given his services to this solitary but active little church on Winchelsea Beach . . .* On August bank holiday Fr John Legg, *in a white cassock, sat outside St. Richard's Church to receive gifts and donations to help pay off the outstanding building debt . . . Between the early hours of the morning and midnight, contributions came equally generously from visitors and residents, the last donation of £1 coming at 11.45 p.m. to make the day's total £67-8-0.*

Fr Legg was assisted by a group of young people. On 21 August a fête was held in the garden of *Harbour Bank* where a further £120 was raised for Church funds and £13 for the Youth Club. Fr Legg ran the Youth Club in the old church building on Dogs Hill Road.

[79] *St Richard's Church in 2005* (Robin Bevis)

Mention has already been made of the uncomfortable position of Winchelsea Beach lying within the parishes of Rye Harbour and Pett. We have seen a press report in Winchelsea Museum said to be dated 1950, which refers to a public meeting to try and reconcile the feelings of the two factions, one of which supported Rye Harbour and the other Pett. The Vicar of Rye Harbour had, apparently, been holding services in Merrivale Hall. The Vicar of Rye Harbour in a letter read to the meeting gave notice that he refused consent for any other Church of England clergyman to usurp his functions in any part of his parish and that he intended to establish a place of worship at Winchelsea Beach as soon as possible. The dispute seems to have rumbled on. In November 1961 the Church Committee wrote to the Archdeacon of Hastings that it was the unanimous wish that St Richard's be placed within the Parish of Winchelsea. The Committee added that initiation and development of work on St Richard's had been done with the support of Winchelsea, not of Rye Harbour. By early 1964 the situation had further deteriorated. The Chairman, officers and members of the Church Committee sent a letter to the Bishop of Chichester expressing concern about *the future of our Church and the Community it hopes to serve*. When Revd John Legg married Hugh Sutton and Lynne Daly at St Richard's Church on 3 September 1966 he certified that it was agreed that, pending full investigation, *St. Richard's should be regarded as if it were in the Parish of Pett notwithstanding anything to the contrary.*

A little over two months later on 11 November 1966 the Church Commissioners laid before Her Majesty in Council a Scheme *for altering the boundaries of the parishes of Pett; Winchelsea; Icklesham; and The Holy Spirit, Rye Harbour, all in the diocese of Chichester.* The Scheme is set out in dense prose and means little without reference to the map accompanying it. *Her Majesty, by and with the advice of Her said Council,* [was] *pleased hereby to confirm the said Scheme*, which became effectual in law upon the publication of the Order in the London Gazette on 17 November 1966.[71] The Church of St Thomas, Winchelsea, became the mother church of St Richard's, Winchelsea Beach.

We can only get a glimpse of the story of St Richard's from the records; those who were active in the Church at the time would have much to tell. Miss Biddle left the Beach in early 1965 and died in 1971. Melville Chaning-Pearce (Diocesan Lay Reader and Chairman of the St Richard's Church Committee), resident of Winchelsea, took (if we have counted accurately) 130 services at St Richard's or at *Harbour Bank* between July 1955 and March 1964. He left Winchelsea in 1964 and died in 1972. A little garden and a handsome bench seat in memory of Melville Chaning-Pearce and his wife were given by their son and placed on the north side of St Richard's. The seat, vandalised in 2003 and then repaired, now stands by the west porch of the Church of St Thomas, Winchelsea. Despite the support of residents of, and visitors to, the Beach, it seems doubtful whether St Richard's would have been built, without the energy and conviction of Miss Biddle and Melville Chaning-Pearce.

12

Rye Harbour Nature Reserve

The Reserve (RHNR) covers an area of 326 ha (nearly 800 acres). The whole of it is on the doorstep of Winchelsea Beach. It is in two distinct, although almost adjoining, parts: the Beach Reserve and Castle Water and Farm.

The western end of the Beach Reserve is at Dogs Hill, where the gate controls the entrance to the Environment Agency private road. Access to the Reserve (on foot) is open along the Agency's road. Despite discouraging notices, the Beach Reserve is accessible by bicycle provided sea-defence works are not in progress with lorries going to and fro; these movements take place in the winter but not at weekends. The map [80] shows that the Beach Reserve extends right down to the Rother and Rye Harbour.

Castle Water is accessible from Morlais Ridge or from the hair-pin bend on Sea Road (see [80]) following footpaths that are way-marked but not as clearly as they might be. From the Castle Water hide a footpath leads to Camber Castle and thence to the Rye Harbour road via the extreme north-east end of the Water.

In 1970 the County Council declared 101 ha (some 250 acres) of beach owned by the Kent River Authority a Local Nature Reserve to be administered by a Management Committee. In 1992 Castle Water and its surrounding land (88 ha or some 215 acres) were purchased by Sussex Wildlife Trust and were brought into the Reserve in the following year. In addition to the Beach Reserve and Castle Water, additions have been made to the Reserve by arrangement with neighbouring landowners, bringing the total area to 326 ha.

Although there is ready access to both the Beach Reserve and Castle Water from Winchelsea Beach, information about the Reserve can only be obtained at the Rye Harbour end. The Reserve's Information Centre is at Lime Kiln Cottage (see [80]) which is less than 10 minutes walk from the free car-park at the Harbour. The Centre is manned by volunteers; it has excellent video displays and a wealth of information in pamphlets, books and cards.

The Reserve is managed and administered by a Management Committee set up by East Sussex County Council with wide representation from the local authorities, the

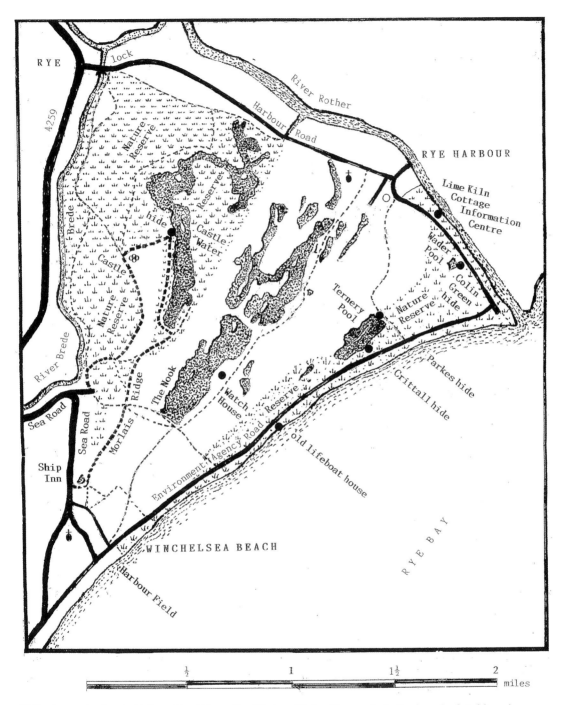

[80] *A map showing the bird-watching hides on Rye Harbour Nature Reserve; footpaths shown by dotted lines, but access from Winchelsea Beach to the Castle Water hide is shown in bolder type* (Clive Chizlett based on an RHNR Plan)

Environment Agency, Sussex Wildlife Trust, RSPB, Sussex Ornithological Society, British Association for Shooting and Conservation and the Friends of Rye Harbour Nature Reserve. The aim of the Committee is to manage the Reserve in such a way that the populations of rare and endangered species are safeguarded and the scenic attraction of the whole area is enhanced. The Reserve must not be seen as the estate of wildlife experts; it is a priceless asset to be enjoyed by all who are prepared to follow the basic rules and conventions for its preservation. One of the formal objectives of the Management Committee is to encourage public appreciation of the area's wild life and scenic value. In 2004 more than 18,000 people visited Lime Kiln Cottage. This is some measure of public interest in the Reserve.

Much of the momentum behind the Reserve is provided by the Friends, who number more than 1700. The Friends was founded in 1973 as a fund-raising branch of the Management Committee; it sets up working parties, provides materials, tools, fencing, and publications; it has contributed to the cost of vehicles and staff. The Friends paid a quarter of the cost of the purchase of Castle Water. The Friends took on the lease and the modernisation of Lime Kiln Cottage and have provided matching funds for various large grants. One such project came from English Nature with funding from Defra's Aggregates Levy Sustainability Fund (ALSF). ALSF provides resources to help tackle a wide range of issues in areas affected by the extraction of aggregates in the form of sand and gravel.

[81] *Ringed plover* (RHNR)

[82] *Oystercatcher* (RHNR photo)

The Reserve is dominated by its proximity to the sea. Apart from the sea and the shingle ridges which the sea has created, water is the most obvious feature of the Reserve's landscape in the form of the Ternery and Wader Pools on the Beach Reserve, and Castle Water. All three are man-made. Ternery Pool and Castle Water are both the outcome of the extraction of shingle for aggregate in years gone by. Extraction, which might be seen as spoliation, has left assets providing habitats and breeding grounds for water-loving birds and stop-overs for migrating flocks. Nature, year by year, has healed the scars and created new life. Man has enhanced it by management and by careful and imaginative construction of islands within the pools and by the profiling of their surrounds. Two hides overlook the Ternery Pool; both Castle Water and the Wader Pool have a hide. All four hides are open freely to visitors; all hides have wheel-chair access but currently only the Crittall Hide overlooking Ternery Pool is 'fully accessible'.

Throughout the year there is much to be seen on the Reserve. It is in the late spring and early summer that there is spectacular activity with breeding colonies of rare little tern, common tern and sandwich tern; the last two nest on the islands of Ternery Pool where they are safe (almost) from depredations by foxes and badgers and where they seem to accept the security afforded by the dense population of black-headed gull.

The little tern perversely nests and raises its young on the open beach protected only by the camouflage of the pebbles and by the benevolent eyes of the Reserve's volunteers. Ground nesting birds such as ringed plover, oystercatcher, redshank, lapwing and wheatear have increased in number and in breeding success. The bittern can be seen, with any amount of luck, in winter in the reed beds of Castle Water; whimbrel are plentiful in April and May.

Some people, residents and visitors, may find the extensive fences along the Beach Reserve forbidding and unfriendly. The protection of so many ground-nesting birds makes this fencing necessary. Without this protection the abundant foxes and badgers would soon make this stretch of coast useless for breeding birds, as has happened on most beaches on the south coast of England.

Although water and the shallow margins are the attraction for so many species of birds, it is the apparent absence of water which strangely provides a hospitable environment for certain plants which thrive on the open beach. The beach reserve has one of the finest examples of coastal vegetation in the country.

In the second half of May and the first half of June the beach along the Environment Agency road becomes a mass of flower. There are white mounds of sea kale, avenues of pink and red valerian, clumps of yellow horned poppy, carpets of sea pea

[83] *Sea kale. Cliff End and the Fairlight cliffs in the background* (RHNR photo)

and little mats of stonecrop, birdsfoot trefoil and herb robert; by contrast there are frequent stands of the deep blue viper's bugloss.

The Reserve is there for everyone. What can be seen is due to good management backed up by working parties of volunteers recruited from the Friends. There must be few coastal areas in south-east England where so much can be seen in peace and quiet and away from traffic. Winchelsea Beach should see itself as a stake-holder in the Reserve. As this is being written (early in 2006) the Environment Agency has completed a secondary flood defence bund extending from near Dogs Hill to the Harbour. The bund is built from soil from the land over which it passes leaving a number of scrapes holding water which will provide more pools reflecting light and colour and attracting yet more bird life. This will add to the security and beauty of the framework within which the village is placed.

Every year in the breeding season from May to August, the Reserve has a caravan placed near the shore adjacent to the area where little tern decide to settle. This is manned from dawn to dusk by volunteer wardens. To take the early morning shift (after the initial trauma of the 4 a.m. alarm clock) and watch the dawn come up and the Reserve come to life is an experience not easily forgotten.

13

The Community and its Association

The word 'community' is more often used by the outside observer in referring to a small group of people living in idyllic or isolated conditions or facing adversity. The adjective 'close-knit' is standard. It has been a fashionable political word, often used as a lever to procure resources or as a reason for providing them. Isolation, adversity, danger or pioneering result in a common experience that brings people together. Take away that adversity or threat, or remove that feeling of starting something new, and the sense of unity and of mutual concern tends to disappear.

Any sense of community that existed amongst the labour force working on the New Harbour or the Martello Towers was probably short-lived. It was probably strong amongst the coastguards, whether they were in the Towers, in their own cottages or in The Ship Inn with whisky at 4d. a quarter. With the colonisation of the Beach after the 1914–1918 war this sense of community emerged. People owned their own plots. They helped one another and in the absence of essential services *plotland communities devised their own solutions.*[72]

The break-through of the sea in the late 1920s, 1930 and 1931 necessitated co-operative effort and mutual support. The establishment of St Richard's Church in the late 1930s owed much to the initiative of Revd Moxon, the Rector of Pett, but was only made possible by the enthusiasm of some of the local community. The 1939–1945 war and the evacuation of Winchelsea Beach broke up this sense of community, but peace, and the return to the Beach, probably re-established it in the face of hardship and the need for repairs and re-establishment after a period of neglect.

Winchelsea Beach has, since the 1920s, been a holiday resort. Since World War II a new dimension has been given to the holiday-making population by the establishment of the caravan parks; Rye Bay Caravan Park started in 1955. In 2001 there were over a 1000 caravan pitches at the Beach[73] including those for tourers. In holiday times and weekends there can be an influx of more than 3000 people. Between the residents (numbering about 1040 in 2001) and holiday makers there is unlikely to be the same community of feeling and outlook. Having said that, it cannot be too strongly emphasised that the establishment of St Richard's Church and the provision of

Winchelsea Beach Community Hall and its facilities owe much to the generosity of the visitors and holiday-home owners and to their willingness to participate in activities sponsored by the Winchelsea Beach Community Association (WBCA), or by charities using the WBCA facilities.

Winchelsea Beach Women's Institute (WI) was formed on 28 March 1952 and had its first meeting on 15 April; in those early days the Institute had over 50 members. It is believed that there was a Winchelsea Beach Residents Association (WBRA) as early as 1930; no early records of the Association have been discovered, but in April 1930 when a delegation met Winchelsea Corporation in an attempt to persuade it to set up an appeal for funds to finance measures to stop the break-through of the sea, the formal reply was sent to the 'Dog's Hill Residents Association'. The WI and WBRA were the focal points for community action and co-operation. Winchelsea Beach did not have a formal voice on Icklesham Parish Council until April 1952, when the Beach became a Ward of the Council. A common purpose, the provision of a village hall, as a centre for the community, drew the WI and WBRA together.

There were difficulties arising from the clash of personalities, the protection of personal interests and the inevitable problems facing a group of public-spirited people confronted or frustrated from time to time by remote organisations, local authorities and public services. WBRA provided a channel of communication and representation. WBRA (and later WBCA) had its own Welfare Officer (Mrs Irene Craddock) whose reports were taken at every committee meeting; she kept in touch with the elderly and those at risk and ensured that the Association sent messages of sympathy when there were bereavements in the village. It takes little imagination to list the sort of problems that appeared before its Committee; planning developments, blocked drains, dirty ditches, dirty water, road subsidences, condition of toilets, dog fouling, low-flying aircraft, unauthorised landing of helicopters.

WBRA assumed responsibility for safety on the shore, a significant issue in view of the number of summer visitors coming to the Beach. A Beach Precautions Committee was set up. There was no lifeboat between Dungeness and Hastings at that time. The Rye Harbour in-shore lifeboat was not set up until 1966. By 1959 WBRA had erected a lifeboat house on land rented from Battle RDC; the boat was manned by volunteers; not until 1964 was an engine bought for the boat. Kent River Board cut a 12ft gap in the wave screen to facilitate launching.

A Newsletter for 1970 recorded that WBRA owned, maintained and voluntarily manned this boat, which provided a valuable service for the benefit of residents and visitors. In May 1974 permission was given for the coastguards to use the boat, presumably because of difficulty in finding volunteers to man it. By June 1984 the lifeboat house had become an eyesore; the boat had not been used in the past year. WBCA decided in March 1985 that the Pett rescue boat could cover the area and that the boat and engine could be sold. The lifeboat house was removed in July 1986.

[84] *The lifeboat named after John Wilkinson who drowned at Dogs Hill*

[85] *The lifeboat crew and a young man who had been rescued on 17 July 1964; left to right: Frank Cheese, Charlie Kerry, Robert Morton (rescued), Terry Myers, Eric Phillips* (Terry Myers)

The village will long remember the initiative and public spirit of a few residents in the winter of 1983 when the Beach (in common with many other communities) felt the effect of industrial action by workers of Southern Water Authority. Something of the story we have been able to get from press reports and residents of that time. On 10 February the strike was already in its third week and the Beach's supply of tap water had been cut off since the end of January. The Authority provided bowsers and volunteers towed them around the village, a necessary remedy in a long straggling village in mid-winter. The water in the bowsers froze overnight. The Authority put locks on the bowsers on the grounds that some people had complained that the bowsers were not there when they came to collect water. The volunteers calling themselves *The Sutton Water Authority* on operation *thirst-aid* brought in tractors and

[86] *'Operation thirst-aid', February 1983, and members of the alternative water authority mending the broken water-main* (Lynne Sutton)

trailers to carry water containers from Rye around the village each evening. On 16 February the volunteers mended a burst water-main, but success was short lived. On 18 February the supply of tap water was restored by the *Authority* after a length of 10 inch pipe had been imported from Belgium.

The Authority, as was to be expected, warned of the possible effects of the measures taken by the volunteers and threatened *issue of proceedings*. On 7 March the Authority informed consumers that the *official repair of the burst water-main had been carried out*.

It was the provision of the village hall that increasingly occupied the attention of WBRA and the WI and led to a labyrinth of committees, which did not always communicate with each other. It seems that WBRA started a fund for a village hall as early as 1948. A Hall Committee, composed of WBRA and WI members, met on 23 July 1966. A number of sites were in mind including that of Merrivale Hall but were too small. It transpired that the Piper family were prepared to sell a plot of land opposite Uncle's Stores and this eventually became the site of the Community Hall. It was not until July 1970 that the site was acquired for £150 and placed in the hands of Trustees.

The realities of providing a village hall were well set out at a meeting of WBRA in April 1972. The land acquired was tied for a Community Association; grants depended on whether the building would provide for major youth usage; the building had to be brick and tile, or a Colt-type building.; the cost would be of the order of £9000 to £10,000. Something of a crisis developed. There were many resignations, including that of the Chairman. The meeting of 11 May 1972, according to the Minutes, *broke down in chaos*. Reason thankfully emerged. In February 1973 WBRA and WI appointed a Steering Committee with terms of reference *to bring into existence the Winchelsea Beach Community Association*. The Association had its inaugural meeting on 11 April 1973. There is a blank in the records for some five years. Not until 2 October 1979 was the Chairman able to report to a public meeting that planning permission had been obtained for the Hall and WBCA was registered as a charity. A Colt-type building was favoured at an estimated cost of £14,000 or £7,000 if the work were done mainly by volunteers.

In November 1979 the *Sussex Express* reported that Icklesham Parish Council had turned down a plea for help and refused a grant of £500. The opinion of a Winchelsea Member was that Winchelsea Beach people should find the money themselves. And they did. It seems that it was in 1979 that fund raising began in earnest. We have been told that it was very hard work and at least one activist remembers that the project for the Hall at times seemed to take over her life. There were social evenings, coffee mornings, jumble sales and fêtes and bonfire/fireworks evenings. On 12 August 1979 Brian Rist, landlord of The Ship, Jim Tremholm, Tony Waters, Steven Craig-Ward and 'Jumbo' Simpson raised £400 for the Hall by a sponsored parachute jump.

In April 1980 WBCA had over £10,000 in hand and work was in progress; volunteers were fortified by the supply of tea and cakes daily from a kind and public-spirited resident.

In June 1980, an East Sussex County Council (ESCC) Community Worker was able to report that WBCA had been rejuvenated over the past year and had made astonishing progress in raising sufficient funds to enable it to order the building; he referred to a thriving small community with a fairly young and active population; there were he said 150 five- to 16-year-olds. On his recommendation ESCC gave £200 to glaze the shell of the hall.

In February 1981 WBRA transferred all property, assets and liabilities to WBCA. The Hall rapidly became a success; two extensions were made in 1982 and 1984. Spring and autumn flower shows and competitions were organised by the Horticultural Society. Annual fetes were instituted; short-mat bowling was started and was well supported. There was table-tennis and a Youth Club was formed.[74]

Despite these initiatives, something of local community effort diminished. The Association is increasingly dependent on the dedication of the few; on the Association's Committee for the time being, rather than on the energy and enthusiasm

[87] *The Community Hall, December 2005* (Robin Bevis)

[88] *WBCA Christmas party for the over-60s* (Sue Chetwood)

of the many. The management of the Hall and the care of its facilities and amenities have become the main priority. The challenges of pioneering have gone. The WI was disbanded on 12 November 2002 after 50 years of enjoyable and valuable activity. In the course of the 1990s the Horticultural Society came to an end.

In the 1950s the village was re-establishing itself as a settled community. Main water came to the Beach in April 1955, and the main sewerage system became operative in August 1959. Even now in 2006 the only roads for which the local authority is responsible are Sea Road, Pett Level Road and Dogs Hill Road; all other roads or tracks are the responsibility of the local residents.

Mention must be made of two assets which have come into the hands of the community. Harbour Field is a major feature of the village and a priceless asset; it is of course a reminder of the New Harbour of Rye. By a Conveyance dated 24 June 1971 there was conveyed to Icklesham Parish Council *a parcel of land of a little over 8 acres known as Harbour Field.* The preamble to the Conveyance stated that the Grantors *are desirous of vesting such property in the Council in Trust for the perpetual use thereof by the public for exercise and recreation as an Open Space.* At the north end of the field is a plaque bearing the inscription: *This field was given to the Parish Council in 1971 by the children of the late Basil and Isabel Holmes in memory of their parents' lifelong work in the preservation of open spaces for the enjoyment of the public.* Isabella Holmes was a niece of William Gladstone; Basil Holmes was Mayor of Winchelsea in 1925. The use to which the Parish Council has allowed the Field to be put has not been without anxieties; the village will need to exercise constant vigilance to ensure that the intentions of the Holmes family are observed, in spirit as well as the letter.

The second acquisition was a field of a little over 20 acres in front of Morlais Ridge. In the summer of 1995 the field was advertised for sale by auction. Colin Hammond wrote that *a few of the residents gathered together to discuss the possibility of raising enough money to buy the field so that preservation of the flora and fauna as well as walking access for local people was maintained.*[75] In a few weeks £30,000 had been given by local residents. On 19 September four residents attended the public auction in London; their bid was successful. The Morlais Trust for Nature Conservation was formed to care for the field and its future.

As we write this in the spring of 2006, the word 'community' is in busy circulation. A body of opinion in Winchelsea has pressed for separate Parish Council status for Winchelsea and its secession as a Ward of Icklesham Parish Council. Amongst the key points that have been expressed in support of a separate Parish Council for Winchelsea, is that it matches the criterion that a Parish should reflect a small, distinctive and recognisable community of interest; it accepts that each of the other three Wards (Icklesham, Rye Harbour and Winchelsea Beach) matches it as well. The particular distinctive features of the Town, its own sense of identity and the strong awareness of the privilege of living in such a beautiful place are emphasised. By contrast, Winchelsea Beach, the protagonists assert, is a *relatively recent ribbon development, that has become a dormitory for Rye and Hastings. A vital contribution to its sustainability as a community is made by the tourism generated by the beach and the large caravan sites . . .* Those who worked so hard at the Beach before and after the 1939–1945 war to support and serve the community might be disappointed by this assessment.

14

The Future

The days when Rye Bay, and our area within it, were a first line of defence against invasion have long gone. The possibility of another new harbour for Rye to the west of the Rother can be dismissed. Dramatic changes as a result of fortification or harbour works can be set aside; changes as a result of social demand are a different matter.

Winchelsea Beach is fortunately placed. Bordered by the sea, it lies in part within the High Weald Area of Outstanding Natural Beauty and much of the surrounding area is a Site of Special Scientific Interest. To the east Rye Harbour Nature Reserve spreads over land owned by the Environment Agency and Sussex Wildlife Trust. There is also land held by the Morlais Trust for Nature Conservation. Nature conservation and concern for the environment command wide support and political backing. Protection of the setting within which the village is placed seems secure. This protection enhances its value and the quality of life within it.

Despite housing demand in the south-east, and around Ashford in particular, it seems unlikely in both the short and long term that the Beach will be greatly affected. In January 2003 Rother District Council wrote that it would not favourably consider housing proposals outside existing development areas.[76] The development boundaries of the Beach are clearly shown in the *Rother District Local Plan – Revised Deposit November 2003*. These boundaries follow existing housing areas with the exception of The Ridge and Morlais Ridge. The Plan allows new dwellings or the placing of caravans at Victoria Way and on land south of Harbour Farm provided such development forms *part of a comprehensive scheme offering significant environmental improvements* including access and drainage. The Plan suggests that the previous policy for the Ridges restricting development to one-for-one replacement will be revised. The Plan, after due process of consultation and the Inspector's report, was passed in July 2006.

In the long term it seems unlikely that there will be major development of housing and amenities, partly because of the conservation and environmental considerations, and partly because so much of the area is designated, for planning purposes, as 'flood plain', which would suggest unsuitability for housing development.

The number of permanent residents at the Beach is likely to increase as it has done over the last few decades.[77] Demand for property may be tempered by lack of employment opportunities locally and by its relative remoteness. But the peculiar attractions of the Beach, its informality, its proximity to the sea and its protected setting, will appeal to many people particularly those contemplating, or reaching, retirement.

Alongside the settled resident population is the flux of holiday makers. The Beach is a holiday area in three ways – for those who have holiday or second homes, for those who have caravans and for day visitors. It was estimated that in 2001 12½ per cent of the dwellings at the Beach were holiday or second homes.[78] This proportion is a considerable reduction on the 1987 estimate of 40%.[79] If the number of permanent residents increases, given the very limited increase in the number of dwellings, the proportion of holiday homes may fall further. The scope for additional caravan pitches seems limited. The capacity of Winchelsea Beach to receive day visitors who arrive by car is limited; the absence of an extensive car-park is a deterrent.

There is a sort of balance between the holiday visitors and the permanent residents. We do not see that balance being disturbed by an overwhelming increase in the number of visitors. The Beach will retain its attraction for those who are content to make their own pleasures by their own efforts.

It is the sea that in the end will dictate what happens on the land which borders it. The sea-wall is our frontier. We are warned of 3°C increase in temperatures in the

[89] *The Wave* (Rye Harbour Nature Reserve)

next 100 years and a rise in sea-levels of 4 mm a year. The implications of these changes are beyond our reach.

The village of Winchelsea Beach may change in appearance and style but not in its setting. The sea has made it and can unmake it. Ethel Macgeorge writing nearly 75 years ago was unrestrained in her enthusiasms. Perhaps we may end with her words:[80]

Ah! The bay with its sparkling mirth, its foaming danger, its changing colours bathed in Sussex sunshine and Sussex shadow . . . here is magic in that bay, and well there may be, for few spots in England can tell such a history of come and gone.

[89] Photo by Pat Littleboy

Notes

1. John Everett Millais (1829–1896).
2. East Sussex Record Office (ESRO) DR/B/116 (Rye RDC) DR/B/94 (Hastings RDC).
3. See Graham Mayhew *Tudor Rye* (University of Sussex 1987), p. 235.
4. *The Journeys of Celia Fiennes* ed. Christopher Morris (Cresset Press 1947); footnote, p. 138.
5. *The Journeys . . . op.cit.,* p. 138.
6. *A Tour through the Whole Island of Great Britain* ed. G. D. H. Cole (J. M. Dent & Son 1962), p. 130.
7. K. M. E. Murray *The Constitutional History of the Cinque Ports* (Manchester U.P. 1935), pp. 207–208.
8. Coventry Kersey Patmore (1823–1896) poet and assistant in the book department of the British Museum. His article *The Fishing Village* for *St. James Gazette* reproduced in Journal 55 of Rye Museum & Local History Group.
9. Malcolm Pratt *Winchelsea – A Port of Stranded Pride* (1998) and *Winchelsea – The Tale of a Medieval Town* (2005) (both published by the author).
10. Jill Eddison's book was published by Tempus in 2000; also see her piece *Catastrophic Changes: a Multi-disciplinary Study of the Evolution of the Barrier Beaches of Rye Bay* Oxford University Committee for Archaeology Monograph No. 46, 1998, pp. 65–87. We are indebted to Jill Eddison for the material on beach barriers and salt-marsh development.
11. See Captain H. Lovegrove *Old Shore Lines near Camber Castle* (The Geographical Journal Vol. CX1X, Part 2, June 1953).
12. See Graham Mayhew *Tudor Rye* (University of Sussex 1987), tables 36 and 43 on pp. 235 and 255.
13. ESRO 99 2-4.
14. ESRO 47/49.
15. ESRO 47/50/8.
16. ESRO ACC 6394.
17. See Dr Sarah Bendall's article *Sixteenth Century Maps of Romney Marsh* in *Imago Mundi* No. 47.
18. Sloane 3233 F3 King's Maritime 111.67 in the Map Room of the Printed Books Department of the British Library.
19. We are grateful to Malcolm Pratt for telling us of this entry in the *House of Commons Journal* dated 3 May 1701.
20. In this chapter there are many references to the Rye Harbour Commissioners; their reports, decisions and attitudes are in their Minutes held at East Sussex Record Office ref. KRA 1 1/1/2.
21. See Paul Monod *The Murder of Mr. Grebell* (Yale University 2003), pp. 226–232.
22. 2 Geo.III c.85.
23. John Meryon *Account of the Origin and Formation of the Harbour of Rye* 1842.
24. 4 Geo.III c.72.
25. John Collard *A Maritime History of Rye* (1978), pp. 38 and 39.

26. John Meryon *op.cit.* section 3, pp. 45 and 46.
27. 37 Geo.III c.130.
28. See A. Saunders *Fortress Britain* (Beaufort 1989), pp.35–37.
29. Saunders *op.cit.*, pp. 40–44.
30. PRO WO44 piece 52.
31. William Cobbett *Rural Rides* first published 1830 (Penguin Books 1967), p. 192.
32. See Sheila Sutcliffe *Martello Towers* (David and Charles 1972).
33. PRO WO55 piece 778.
34. PRO WO44 piece 53.
35. PRO WO44 piece 282.
36. Peter Schenk *Invasion of England 1940 – The Planning of Operation Sealion* (Conway Maritime Press 1990), pp. 270–286, 346–349; Richard Overy *The Battle* (Penguin Books 2000) pp. 68, 80, 87, 95–98; Martin Marix Evans *Invasion – Operation Sealion 1940* (Pearson Education 2004), pp. x, 71, 85, 92–93, 98, 191–204.
37. AJP Taylor *English History 1914–1945* (Oxford 1965), pp. 486–487.
38. AJP Taylor *op.cit.*, p. 489.
39. Plan entitled *The Intended New Harbour copied by Wm. Stocks in 1839* on a scale of 1 inch to 100 ft.; the original must have been drawn in about 1756. The plan was salvaged and is, at present, in private ownership.
40. R.F. Dell ed. *Winchelsea Corporation Records.* ESCC 1963, schedule Nos. 242, 294–300, 347, 348.
41. Pamela Haines's Introduction to *East Sussex Census – 1851 Index* compiled by C.J. Barnes.
42. Iain Finlayson *Writers in Romney Marsh* (Severn House Publishers 1986), p. 15.
43. For both of these quotes and for background on artists and authors in Winchelsea, we are indebted to Malcolm Pratt and Chapter 17 of his *Winchelsea – A Port of Stranded Pride*
44. ESRO DR/B/94/3.
45. *Victoria County History* (VCH) Sussex IX, p. 177.
46. Joyce Wheatley in *Sussex History* No. 24, 1987, pp. 20–22, obituary in *The Temperance Record* 23 January 1875 and *Bygone Rye Harbour* Rye Memories Vol. 18.
47. Dennis Hardy and Colin Ward *Arcadia for All – The Legacy of a Makeshift Landscape* (Mansell 1984).
48. The Minutes of the two RDCs are held in ESRO: Rye DR/B/116/7, 8 and 9; Hastings DR/B/94/5, 6 and 7.
49. Ethel Macgeorge *The Story of Two Ancient Towns Winchelsea and Rye* (Adams and Son Rye 1932), p.90
50. *Rye Memories* no.16 (The Thomas Peacocke School Local History Group 1991), pp.64-66
51. The Minutes of the Battle RDC Buildings and Planning Committee for the period 1934 to 20 June 1940 are held in ESRO DR/B/12/1–4
52. *Dalton's Weekly House and Apartment Advertiser*, 8 May 1937, quoted by Hardy and Ward *op.cit.*, p. 58.
53. Hardy and Ward *op.cit.*, p. 34.
54. Jill Eddison *op.cit.,* pp. 123, 124.
55. Public Record Office (PRO) WO55 piece 2270 Pett, 1870–1923.
56. PRO MAF 49/308.
57. ESRO DR/B/116/8.
58. We are indebted to the Corporation of Winchelsea and to Malcolm Pratt, the Clerk to the Corporation, for permission to quote from the Corporation's records.
59. PRO MAF 49/308.
60. *Morning Post* 20 July 1933.

61. Frank Midmer and George Roberts *Sea Defence and Land Drainage of Romney Marsh* Oxford Univesity Committee for Archaeology Monograph No. 21, 1988, p. 163.

62. John N.C. Taylor *Pett in Sussex* (Edgerton Publishing Services 2004).

63. Most of the extracts from the press reports have been taken from material held by Winchelsea Museum.

64. Geoff Hutchinson *The Mary Stanford Disaster* first published 1984, revised edition 1993.

65. Richard Tollett *Mary Stanford – The Story of a Lifeboat* Rye Harbour Newsletter, Issue 3, vol. 4, 2004.

66. *The Lifeboat* Vol.XXVII, No. 297, pp. 203–205.

67. *Ibid,* p. 196.

68. Geoff Hutchinson *op.cit.*, pp. 15–17.

69. *The Lifeboat* vol.XXVII, No.297, p. 198.

70. ESRO PAR 543.

71. We are grateful to the Church Commissioners (Pastoral Division) for seeking out and sending us a copy of the Order-in-Council embodying the Scheme.

72. Hardy and Ward *op.cit.*, p. 28.

73. The figures for the number of caravan pitches and population are in a letter from Planning Strategy, Rother District Council to MVS, dated 20 June 2005.

74. Much of the foregoing has been drawn from the records of WBRA and WBCA and press material of the time. We are grateful to the Chairman and Committee of WBCA for permission to use these records and for the loan of the press material.

75. Colin Hammond's Foreword to Patricia Littleboy's booklet *The Morlais Trust for Nature Conservation*.

76. *Towards a Planning Strategy for Rother District* January 2003, p. 30, para. 27.

77. Para. 6 of the 1987 Village Policy recorded that the permanent population was estimated to be 650 in 1981 and 520 in 1971. In 2001 the estimate was 1040.

78. Letter from Planning Strategy, Rother District Council, to MVS dated 20 June 2005.

79. *Winchelsea Beach – Village Policy 1987 –* Rother District Council, para. 6.

80. Ethel Macgeorge *op.cit.*, pp. 19 and 20.

Index